Policy Choices

Michigan State University Press
East Lansing, Michigan 48823-5202

Michigan State University Institute for Public Policy and Social Research Public Policy Series

03 02 01 00 99 98 97 96 95 1 2 3 4 5 6 7 8 9

Library of Congress Cataloging-in-Publication Data

Policy choices : creating Michigan's future / edited by Phyllis T.H. Grummon
    and Brendan P. Mullan.
        p.   cm. — (Michigan State University Institue for Public Policy
    and Social Research public policy series)
    Includes bibliographical references and index.
    ISBN 0-87013-382-9
    1. Political planning—Michigan. 2. Michigan—Politics and government—
1951- 3. Michigan—Population. 4. Agriculture and state—Michigan.
5. Education and state—Michigan. 6. Urban policy—Michigan. I. Grummon,
Phyllis T. H. II. Mullan, Brendan P. III. Series.
JK5849.P64P65 1995
320.9774—dc20   95-10487
                                                                                    CIP

Published with the support of the Institute for Public Policy and Social Research, Michigan State University

Acknowledgements

The editors wish to thank Frani Bickart and Lee Jernstadt of the Institute for Public Policy and Social Research for their efforts in formatting, reading and editing manuscripts, as well as in helping us coordinate communications among the authors and the Editorial Board. As all editors know, it is only with the assistance of people like Frani and Lee that books actually make it "out the door." The Editorial Board wishes to thank Dr. Jack H. Knott, Director of IPPSR, for his continued support in bringing this policy series to fruition.

Contents

III. EDUCATION POLICY

IV. URBAN POLICY

Foreword

The Institute for Public Policy and Social Research at Michigan State University is pleased to be able to offer the second volume in the *Policy Choices* series. The first volume covered a broad range of policy issues, many of which have subsequently risen to prominence in state and national debates, such as health care and school finance. Our goal for the series is to continue to provide those interested in policy issues a place to learn about the range of options available for consideration in making decisions. The editorial board was expanded this year and two members took primary responsibility for shepherding the volume through the publication process. We hope that you continue to find these volumes useful.

Jack Knott
Director
Institute for Public Policy and Social Research

Introduction

This is the second volume in the *Policy Choices* series. As with the first volume, the focus is on providing readers with a perspective on a number of policy issues. The authors have been asked to reflect on the background of these issues, the ways in which other states or countries have addressed the issues, relevant research, and the history and direction of policy options in Michigan. This volume begins, as did the last, by presenting three articles looking at demographic issues in Michigan. The population of Michigan provides a context for thinking about the policies that will be formulated and their effects on its citizens. Three articles in this volume discuss issues related to agriculture and rural populations. This is an area of major concern for Michigan, as the quality of life for many citizens is affected by agriculture and the rural economy. One of the articles has a clear social science focus and examines rural leadership, while the remaining two articles are more entomologically oriented and examine the policy implications of pests and pest management for Michigan agriculture. Educational issues are considered in two papers. One article looks at the ways in which educational reform efforts are affected by other policies, particularly those related to professional development for teachers. The second article reviews the options for building a comprehensive system for aiding the transition from school into the workplace. The final article of the volume reviews the patterns of service delivery in Detroit local communities, individuals, and advocates can play to produce innovative policies at the local level. Specifically, this article examines how local knowledge is influenced by external and internal information sources and how rural agricultural leaders' knowledge can complement the knowledge of institutional scientists and policymakers. Empirical data show that Michigan agricultural leaders have a great deal more contact with fellow leaders and farmers than with external educational, governmental, or agribusiness institutions. Suggested policy recommendations include the development of mechanisms to bring local leaders and policymakers together and for facilitating communication between the two.

Craig Harris and Mark Whalon generalize the discussion of the impact of pest management by choosing to focus on the production of fruits and vegetables and discussing Michigan's agricultural system and the current policies which govern pest management. Following a comprehensive review of current pest management policy in which they delineate the various components that constitute the commodity chain, Harris and Whalon highlight five principal elements of current pest management policy: registered uses, residue tolerances, cosmetic standards, applicator licensing, and research and extension. Conflict among various interest groups and forces of change (e.g. pesticide manufacturers, environmental agencies, growers' associations, consumers) will only continue and increase if pest management strategies continue on their current trajectory. Harris and Whalon refuse to choose between a continuation of present pest management policies and the inevitable alternative short-term solution of crisis management. Rather they advocate an integrated pest management policy that acknowledges the many different approaches and the role they play in pest management: the optimal strategy is to identify the proper role for each. This strategy is the "middle road" alluded to in the title of the paper, and the authors carefully develop the implications of this policy direction for pest management.

In their article, Bryan Pijanowski, Stuart Gage, and Deborah McCullough shift the policy focus to examine an environmental issue with complex consequences: policy issues as they relate to the impacts of an introduced forest pest, the gypsy moth. Key policy issues associated with the Michigan gypsy moth include how to evaluate the impact of this moth on forests, tourism, and urban areas and how to effectively control and manage a forest pest like the gypsy moth. Pijanowski and Gage trace the spread of the pest in terms of defoliation and chemical control efforts. Furthermore, they identify each of the actors and institutions involved in addressing the gypsy moth problem in Michigan (the U.S. and Michigan Departments of Agriculture and Natural Resources and academic institutions) and address their respective roles in creating and enforcing pest management policies. Education, control, and research constitute the major policy initiatives in this area, and this paper highlights weaknesses with each. Echoing concerns voiced in Mullan's article, communication between the key groups involved in forest management programs is essential. Input must be provided to, and feedback received from, the public and environmental organizations. The article concludes with the observation that one possible missing link in the current communication network is the exchange of ideas between policy analysts and researchers at universities. The authors call for the holding of regular meetings and symposia to bring all interested agencies and activists together to accomplish effective policy innovation and implementation.

Section three on educational policy looks at two different, but related, issues. The first article, "State Education Policy and Teaching Practice: Issues Yet to be Joined," suggests that the recent focus on educational reform through law and rule making has left out a key area in actually changing the way education is delivered. Steve Kaagan and Diane Holt-Reynolds describe the range of strategies used to change schools—mandates, binding agreements, incentives, capacity building, and expert opinion. They argue that the latter two, building teachers' capacity to try new educational methods and helping teachers to learn from each other more effectively, have been underutilized as educational reform strategies. They close their piece by suggesting that Michigan policymakers could forge new ground by considering how they could support those strategies in their educational reform efforts.

The second article in the education section reviews efforts to build policies and programs to support "The Transition from School to Work." Phyllis Grummon describes a number of initiatives at the federal and state levels to help high school students move successfully from school into the workplace. Some of these have been integrated with other educational reform efforts, particularly ones that focus on applied learning methods. However, unlike many of our foreign competitors, there is no comprehensive model in the United States for helping students make this transition. In addition, few programs have

Infant Mortality in Michigan: Implications for Public Policy and Scientific Research

Nigel Paneth

INFANT MORTALITY—A POPULAR VIEW OF THE PROBLEM

Infant mortality is widely viewed as an instance of the lack of application of public resources to communities in need. The disparity in infant mortality rates between black and white communities is likewise viewed as a problem that can easily be resolved if only we put our mind to it. A recent editorial in the *Detroit Free Press* forcefully expresses this view:

> Michigan simply must not throw up its hands and treat as an incomprehensible mystery the widening gap between the death rates for black babies and white babies.
>
> The latest statistics released by the state Health Department showed that the gap is getting wider. Among blacks in Michigan, 22.1 of every 1,000 babies die during the first year of life. Among whites, the rate is 8.9 per 1,000. The rate for whites has been going down; the rate for blacks has remained about the same for the last several years.

Those are discouraging numbers, but at some level, they are numbers that can be changed. There are states and countries that do significantly better than we have done at cutting down on the rate of infant death. There are prevention strategies not included in Michigan's arsenal for attacking this problem that will help to overcome the societal problems reflected by the grim statistics.

Indeed, child advocacy groups have been arguing for several years that there are identifiable strategies waiting to be implemented. While it is true that Michigan has tried to throw its infant mortality net somewhat more broadly than some other states, it is also true that there are many areas where effective strategies are known, but have not yet been applied.

The state cannot, of course, wave a wand and make the gap go away. The gap has to include many variables: poverty; the distribution of health care; the prevention strategies the president is attempting to address at the national level; the life-style questions such as alcohol, tobacco and drug use that loom ever larger as determinants of the health of newborns; nutrition. But the public health challenge is, nonetheless, relatively straightforward. If the Michigan community concludes that this gap must be closed, we can begin to close it.

Gov. John Engler, though, has to take as seriously as does his health director, Vernice Davis Anthony, the importance of moving forward with a state prevention strategy. Michigan ultimately pays, one way or the other, for its failure to do better about assuring a healthy start for youngsters of all races.

The cost of most of the identifiable prevention strategies is peanuts compared to the costs of dealing with the failure to put them in place. It isn't a matter of do-gooding or runaway government. It is a matter of mobilizing the machinery of the community, public and private, to deal with a problem that is a matter of life and death.

As Ms. Davis Anthony said in announcing the dreary pattern, "It's unacceptably high. We've got to do more." Those numbers are unacceptably high. They and the tragedy they represent are too important to be dismissed as merely the concern of do-gooders. They are the business of everyone in the state, starting with those, such as the governor, who purport to be our leaders.[1]

In four separate locations the editorial refers to "prevention strategies" or "effective strategies" to lower infant mortality in black communities, but does not specify the strategies it has in mind. Four "life style" issues are identified as important—alcohol, tobacco use, illicit drug use, and nutrition—apparently assuming that these factors are the key determinants of infant mortality and of black-white differences in infant mortality. The editorial seems to take on faith that the really difficult task—implementing effective programs to reduce infant mortality—is simply a matter of conviction and enthusiasm. But as with most intersections of social forces and biology, infant mortality is a more complex and difficult problem than most casual observers realize.

INFANT MORTALITY IN HISTORICAL PERSPECTIVE

Our assumption that there must be a solution out there waiting to be implemented may reflect our experiences with previous public health successes. As we approach the year 2000, we would do well to realize that greater improvements in public health have occurred in this century among industrialized nations than perhaps have ever occurred over the same time period in the recorded history of humankind. Life expectancy in the U.S. improved from 47.3 in 1900 to 75.7 in 1992, largely because infant mortality, 120 per thousand live births in 1900, declined more than ten-fold to 8.7 per thousand in 1992.[2]

What can account for such remarkable changes? Broadly speaking, two phenomena have accounted for virtually all of the progress: improvements in the standard of living for large segments of the population, and the development of public health strategies that have moderated the adverse effects of a low standard of living on people's health. Of these two factors, the first is by far the more important, but the latter has played no small part itself. Early in this century the nature of infant mortality ensured that improvements in standards of living and hygiene would have an important impact. Most infant deaths occurred after the immediate neonatal period, as the infant steadily increased its exposure to the nutritional and microbial hazards of the outside world. As in the Third World today, the main cause of death was infection, primarily intestinal or respiratory, with susceptibility compounded by poor nutrition.

As standards of living increased, infant nutrition improved with resultant improvement in resistance to infection. Diminished crowding, due to better housing and smaller families, was another reflection of better living standards. At the same time, public health played a role in providing safer water and food and in educating the public about optimum nutritional habits and hygienic practices.

INEQUALITIES IN INFANT MORTALITY

Not all communities in the United States, however, have participated equally in the reduction in infant mortality. Information on race-specific infant mortality from the first half of this century is probably unreliable, but more recent trends in infant mortality illustrate these inequalities. Black infant mortality was double that of white infants in 1950, and is still double that of white infants in 1991 (figure 1). Infant mortality has declined in both populations, and the absolute

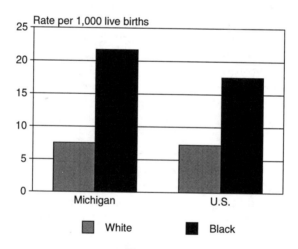

Figure 1.
**Infant Mortality Rates by Race in Michigan and
in the United States, 1991.**

Sources: "Mortality Statistics Branch: Infant Mortality-United States, 1991," *Morbidity and Mortality Weekly Reports* 42 (1993):926-30; Office of the Registrar and Center for Health Statistics, *Michigan Health Statistics* (Lansing: Michigan Department of Public Health, June 1993).

difference between black and white infant death rates has also declined, but relative to each other, the two groups have remained in essentially the same position. In Michigan, disparities in infant mortality between black and white infants are actually higher than for the nation as a whole. By contrast, in 1950 infant mortality in Japan was twice that of the U.S., but in 1990, the positions were reversed, with U.S. infant mortality double that of Japan's.

INFANT MORTALITY TODAY—A DIFFERENT PROBLEM

Can today's policy initiatives have the same impact on infant mortality that public health action had earlier in this century? The answer to this question depends a great deal on our understanding of today's infant mortality problems, which are quite different from those of the first half of this century. Currently, most infant deaths occur in the first weeks of life. Excess risk is not so much due to exposure to the perils of the outside world as it is a reflection of poorly understood events that take place during pregnancy. Two biological phenomena dominate the cause-of-death statistics among infants in the U.S.—premature delivery and congenital malformations. A third cause, Sudden Infant Death Syndrome, accounts for a substantial part of the remainder.

Of the three causes, premature delivery is by far the most important in explaining differences between black and white infant death rates. Prematurity is more than twice as common in the black community. Currently about 17 percent of black infants, and just 8 percent of white infants, are born prior to 37 weeks of gestation (figure 2). These figures have been quite steady for about twenty years—the furthest back it is possible to go because gestational age has only been recorded in most states' birth certificates since the 1970s.

Mortality increases steadily with shorter gestational ages at birth, and the most problematic births are those before 32 weeks of gestation, which are over-represented by at least three-fold in the black community. Moreover, there is some evidence that the racial discrepancy in severe prematurity is worsening. If we use the number of very low birthweight births (infants weighing 1.5 kg or less, about 3 pounds) as a proxy for very early delivery, we find that the rate in the black population has gone from 2 percent of live births in 1960 to close to 3 percent in 1990. In the white population it has remained steady at 1 percent over the thirty-year period.[3] High rates of prematurity also

infants in Michigan (infants weighing less than 1,500 g at birth, virtually all of whom need intensive care) have better access to these services than in most other states.[7]

MICHIGAN PUBLIC HEALTH STRATEGIES FOR THE FUTURE

The recently issued Michigan Department of Public Health strategic plan, entitled *Healthy Michigan 2000*,[8] sets out some of the next steps for public health policy in Michigan in the area of infant mortality. The health department has defined four priority areas for the decade of the 1990s. These are:

1. Influencing health risk behavior
2. Survival of the African-American male
3. Influencing the reduction of adverse environmental and occupational health effects
4. Public Health evolution

Infant mortality continues to be viewed as a high priority health issue. Of the six goals listed under Priority Area 1, two deal directly with infant mortality. These goals are reducing unintended pregnancies (Goal 1.3) and maintaining the decline in infant mortality while minimizing disparities among populations (Goal 1.4).

The focus on preventing unintended pregnancies represents an innovative approach to the infant mortality problem. This focus acknowledges the likely relationship between a woman's lack of control of her reproductive life and her risk of delivering prematurely. Unwanted or unintended pregnancies are unfortunately very common in our society (about 50 percent of live births in the U.S. are the product of unplanned pregnancies), and the population groups with the highest rates of unintended or unwanted pregnancies are also those with high rates of preterm delivery. The deferral of pregnancy into periods of a woman's life when she is more able to undertake the tasks of motherhood will surely have many beneficial consequences over and above any effect on infant mortality. At the same time, many of the mechanisms proposed by the MDPH to reduce unintended pregnancies (e.g. abstinence programs, family planning services) will likely also reduce the impact of sexually transmitted diseases, themselves causes of infant mortality.

The MDPH continues also to support the more conventional approaches to the infant mortality/low birthweight problem by improving access to prenatal care, supporting nutrition education, and developing substance abuse programs. As goals for the year 2000 in Michigan, MDPH has set an overall infant mortality rate of 7.5 per thousand live births, and an African-American infant mortality rate of 14.0 per thousand.

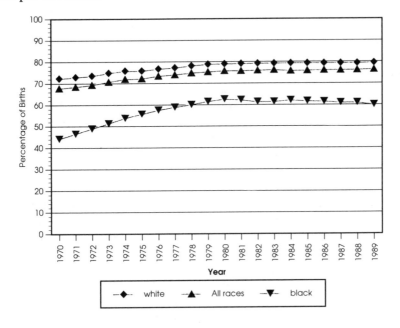

*First prenatal care visit within 3 months of conception (first trimester).

Figure 3.

Time-Trends in First Trimester Prenatal Care Attendance in the United States, by Race, 1970-1990.

Source: National Center for Health Statistics, U.S. Department of Health and Human Services, Advance Report of Final Natality Statistics, 1989. Monthly Vital Statistics Report, vol. 40, no. 8 supplement (Hyattsville, Maryland: Public Health Services, 1991).

Reprinted with Permission of A. D. Racine, T. J. Joyce, and M. Grossman, "Effectiveness of Health Care Services for Pregnant Women and Infants," *The Future of Children* 2 (1993):40-57.

AN EPIDEMIOLOGIC PERSPECTIVE ON CURRENT AND FUTURE PUBLIC POLICY INITIATIVES TO REDUCE INFANT MORTALITY

Unfortunately, there is reason to believe that further development of conventional strategies can make only small improvements in the infant mortality picture. Goal-setting is only as good as the mechanisms available to achieve the goals, and the mechanisms available, when examined closely, have often failed to meet expectations.

Access to prenatal care has expanded in the U.S. during the past two decades (figure 3), and at present, 80 percent of women enter prenatal care in the first trimester of pregnancy, up from less than 70 percent in 1970. Unfortunately, even now only 60 percent of black women enter prenatal care that early, although this is considerably better than the 45 percent figure of 1970. In Michigan in 1991, only 5 percent of pregnant women received less than five prenatal visits.[9] However, the national improvements in early prenatal care attendance have not been accompanied by any change in the national prematurity rate, as a comparison of figures 2 and 3 will show.

Although women who fail to attend prenatal care or who attend very late have worse pregnancy outcomes than women whose prenatal care attendance is prompt and more regular, it is a mistake to attribute all differences in pregnancy outcome to the prenatal care itself. Conventional prenatal care includes no component specifically directed at preventing premature delivery, and no plausible mechanism links prenatal care delivery to changes in the prematurity rate. The significance of prenatal care lies in its role in detecting and treating pregnancy complications such as diabetes and pre-eclampsia, in providing access to diagnostic services such as amniocentesis, in counseling women about health-related behaviors, and in linking women in need to social service agencies. Important as these activities are, none of them has proven effective in preventing prematurity.

The central difficulty is that premature delivery is an intractable problem, poorly understood from the perspectives of laboratory science, epidemiology, or social science. It bears a clear relationship to measures of social class as well as to ethnicity in the U.S. Poorer women are more likely to deliver prematurely, but there are interesting, and perhaps instructive, exceptions. Mexican-American women, whose incomes are considerably lower than those of non-Hispanic whites, have little or no excess of prematurity, nor do Southeast Asian immigrants to the U.S.[10]

Decades of research into the problem of low birthweight have failed to uncover any powerful risk factors for either premature delivery or low birthweight in developed countries. Recent work suggests that cocaine use in pregnancy is associated with prematurity.[11] But is cocaine itself the cause of prematurity or is something else in the life of the cocaine user the real cause? As figure 2 shows, prematurity rates do not appear to have been affected by the massive increase in cocaine use in the 1980s. In two studies of inner city populations, non-cocaine users had prematurity rates of 14-18 percent, double or more the rate among U.S. whites.[12]

As with infant mortality earlier in this century, if socio-economic status improves substantially in the black community, prematurity rates will undoubtedly decline, even though the mechanism by which this improvement comes about remains obscure. But absent understanding of the mechanisms, risk factors, or causes of prematurity, it is impossible to devise effective public health action to shield people from this risk, other than by providing the usual sensible advice to avoid smoking, drinking and illicit drug use, actions which by themselves are not likely to substantially change the prematurity rate.

Public policy includes not only public health action, but also support for the scientific research that underlies public health action. It is necessary to recognize that prematurity is at the heart of our infant mortality problem, and that prematurity cannot be attributed in any simple fashion to specific lifestyles. Rather, we must acknowledge that our understanding of prematurity is very limited, and that a broad program of research is needed into its fundamental biology, its epidemiology, and into the ethnic, social, and psychological contexts in which it occurs. Only then will we be prepared to undertake serious prevention efforts. To its great credit, the MDPH recognizes this problem in its strategic plan for Michigan. Listed as one of its strategies for achieving its infant mortality goals is "collaborate with universities on epidemiological studies of low birthweight, especially among African-American women."

The *Detroit Free Press* admonishes that the difference in infant mortality rates for black and white infants should not be treated as an "incomprehensible mystery." The mistake lies not in considering infant mortality a mystery, only in viewing the mystery as incomprehensible.

NOTES

1. "Infant Death: State Must Do More to Close the Gap," *Detroit Free Press*, 20 August 1993. Reprinted with permission of the *Detroit Free Press*.
2. National Center for Health Statistics, "Annual Summary of Births, Marriages, Divorces, and Deaths: United States, 1992," *Monthly Vital Statistics Report* 41, no. 13 (Hyattsville, Maryland: Public Health Services, 1993).
3. J. C. Kleinman, M. G. Fowler, and S. S. Kessel, "Comparison of Infant Mortality among Twins and Singletons: United States 1960 and 1983," *Am J Epidemiol* 133 (1991): 133-43; National Center for Health Statistics, "Advance Report of Final Natality Statistics, 1991," *Monthly Vital Statistics Report*, 42, suppl., 3 (Hyattsville, Maryland: Public Health Service, 1993).
4. "Mortality Statistics Branch: Infant Mortality-United States, 1991," *Morbidity and Mortality Weekly Reports* 42 (1993):926-30.
5. J. C. Kleinman, "The Slowdown in the Infant Mortality Decline," *Paed Perinat Epidemiol* 4 (1990): 373-81.
6. Public Health Service, *Healthy People 2000: National Health Promotion and Disease Prevention Activities*, DHHS Publication no. [PHS]91-50212 (Washington D.C.: USDHS, PHS, 1991).
7. N. Paneth and M. Rip, "Uses of Epidemiology in the Evaluation of Regional Perinatal Services," *Social & Preventive Medicine* 39 (1994):3-10.
8. Michigan Department of Public Health, *Michigan Department of Public Health, Healthy Michigan 2000* (Lansing: Michigan Department of Public Health, 1993).
9. Michigan League for Human Services, *Kids Count in Michigan* (Lansing: Michigan League for Human Services, 1993).
10. R. Rumbaut and J. Weeks, *Perinatal Risks and Outcomes among Low-Income Immigrants Final Report to Bureau of Maternal and Child Health* (Springfield, Virginia: National Technical Information Service, U.S. Department of Commerce).
11. L. N. Robins and J. L. Mills, "Effects of In Utero Exposure to Street Drugs," *Am J Pub Health*, suppl. 83 (1993):3-34.
12. E. M. Ostrea, M. Brady, S. Gause, et al., "Drug Screening of Newborns by Meconium Analysis: A Large-Scale Prospective Study," *Pediatrics* 89 (1992):107-13; D. A. Bateman, S. K. C. Ng, C. A. Hangen, et al., "The Effects of Intrauterine Cocaine Exposure in Newborns," *Am J Pub Health* 83 (1993):190-93.

Changes in the Distribution of Michigan Family Income

Bettie Landauer-Menchik and Paul Menchik

INTRODUCTION

It is by now well established that the U.S. income distribution—the way in which our national income is divided among the population—has undergone a significant change in the last fifteen to twenty years.[1] While a multiplicity of terms has been used to describe this transformation (i.e., "wage stretching," "withering" of the middle class, income distributions that have become more "dispersed," or more "skewed," or just more unequal), there is no disagreement with this fundamental finding.[2] The most frequently mentioned culprits for this trend include the state of our education system, the decline of the manufacturing sector of our economy, the decline of unionization, the decline in the inflation-adjusted minimum wage, changes in patterns of international trade, technological changes in production, reduced enforcement of anti-bias legislation, changing federal budget priorities, the growth of single-parent households, and changes in the age structure of the population. At this stage it is fair to say that there is no universal agreement on the quantitative importance of these factors.

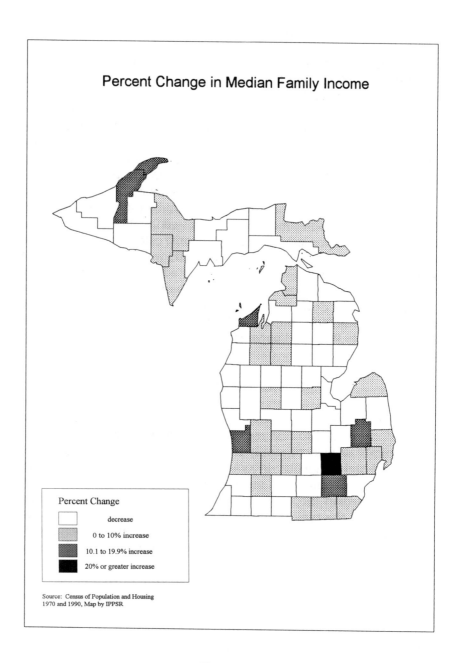

Figure 1.

TABLE 1: TWENTY YEARS OF CHANGE IN FAMILY INCOME GROUPS IN MICHIGAN, 1969-1989

	NUMBER OF FAMILIES IN LOW INCOME GRP 1969	NUMBER OF FAMILIES IN LOW INCOME GRP 1989	CHANGE IN NUMBER OF FAMILIES IN LOW INCOME GROUP 69-89	PERCENTAGE CHANGE IN FAMILIES IN LOW INCOME GROUP 69-89	NUMBER OF FAMILIES IN UPPER INCOME GROUP 1969	NUMBER OF FAMILIES IN UPPER INCOME GROUP 1989	CHANGE IN NUMBER OF FAMILIES IN UPPER INCOME GROUP 69-89	PERCENTAGE CHANGE IN FAMILIES IN UPPER INCOME GROUP 69-89
U.S.	13,303,836	16,223,832	2,919,996	21.9%	10,591,900	19,495,543	8,903,643	84.1%
MICHIGAN	408,749	584,957	176,208	43.1%	584,204	776,215	192,011	32.9%
ALCONA	1,051	1,472	421	40.1%	155	232	77	49.7%
ALGER	644	909	265	41.1%	145	251	106	73.1%
ALLEGAN	3,987	5,231	1,244	31.2%	2,476	5,716	3,240	130.9%
ALPENA	1,957	2,829	872	44.6%	1,026	1,381	355	34.6%
ANTRIM	1,109	1,788	679	61.2%	378	744	366	96.8%
ARENAC	880	1,756	876	99.5%	344	581	237	68.9%
BARAGA	681	842	161	23.6%	181	205	24	13.3%
BARRY	2,228	3,192	964	43.3%	1,586	3,442	1,856	117.0%
BAY	5,255	8,078	2,823	53.7%	6,051	7,782	1,731	28.6%
BENZIE	736	1,320	584	79.3%	265	404	139	52.5%
BERRIEN	9,251	12,174	2,923	31.6%	8,145	10,302	2,157	26.5%
BRANCH	2,392	3,288	896	37.5%	1,481	1,962	481	32.5%
CALHOUN	7,084	10,151	3,067	43.3%	8,544	9,419	875	10.2%
CASS	2,595	3,741	1,146	44.2%	2,019	2,870	851	42.1%
CHARLEVOIX	1,262	1,721	459	36.4%	533	995	462	86.7%
CHEBOYGAN	1,479	2,373	894	60.4%	479	614	135	28.2%
CHIPPEWA	2,946	3,025	79	2.7%	636	1,029	393	61.8%
CLARE	1,737	3,510	1,773	102.1%	449	801	352	78.4%
CLINTON	1,853	2,522	669	36.1%	2,705	5,538	2,833	104.7%
CRAWFORD	552	1,190	638	115.6%	221	384	163	73.8%
DELTA	2,447	3,344	897	36.7%	1,150	1,706	556	48.3%
DICKINSON	1,976	2,194	218	11.0%	635	1,505	870	137.0%
EATON	2,635	4,147	1,512	57.4%	4,864	9,004	4,140	85.1%
EMMET	1,280	1,774	494	38.6%	726	1,322	596	82.1%
GENESEE	17,820	31,356	13,536	76.0%	29,609	36,703	7,094	24.0%
GLADWIN	1,227	2,789	1,562	127.3%	368	758	390	106.0%
GOGEBIC	2,174	2,049	(125)	-5.7%	276	494	218	79.0%
GRAND TRAVE	2,121	3,672	1,551	73.1%	1,718	4,384	2,666	155.2%
GRATIOT	2,445	3,268	823	33.7%	1,521	1,848	327	21.5%
HILLSDALE	2,491	3,391	900	36.1%	1,213	2,113	900	74.2%
HOUGHTON	3,954	3,380	(574)	-14.5%	634	1,031	397	62.6%
HURON	3,192	3,445	253	7.9%	1,039	1,336	297	28.6%
INGHAM	10,682	14,830	4,148	38.8%	16,634	20,936	4,302	25.9%
IONIA	2,335	3,299	964	41.3%	1,741	3,234	1,493	85.8%
IOSCO	2,490	3,530	1,040	41.8%	561	906	345	61.5%
IRON	1,505	1,782	277	18.4%	227	280	53	23.3%
ISABELLA	2,369	3,821	1,452	61.3%	1,461	2,386	925	63.3%
JACKSON	6,411	9,659	3,248	50.7%	8,236	10,214	1,978	24.0%
KALAMAZOO	8,078	11,956	3,878	48.0%	12,149	18,676	6,527	53.7%
KALKASKA	631	1,409	778	123.3%	95	411	316	332.6%

Source: Census of Population and Housing, 1970 and 1990

TABLE 1:TWENTY YEARS OF CHANGE IN FAMILY INCOME GROUPS IN MICHIGAN, 1969-1989

	NUMBER OF FAMILIES IN LOW INCOME GRP 1969	NUMBER OF FAMILIES IN LOW INCOME GRP 1989	CHANGE IN NUMBER OF FAMILIES IN LOW INCOME GROUP 69-89	PERCENTAGE CHANGE IN FAMILIES IN LOW INCOME GROUP 69-89	NUMBER OF FAMILIES IN UPPER INCOME GROUP 1969	NUMBER OF FAMILIES IN UPPER INCOME GROUP 1989	CHANGE IN NUMBER OF FAMILIES IN UPPER INCOME GROUP 69-89	PERCENTAGE CHANGE IN FAMILIES IN UPPER INCOME GROUP 69-89
KENT	18,155	25,156	7,001	38.6%	22,936	40,148	17,212	75.0%
KEWEENAW	369	270	(99)	-26.8%	21	39	18	85.7%
LAKE	749	1,335	586	78.2%	96	182	86	89.6%
LAPEER	2,350	3,854	1,504	64.0%	2,482	6,792	4,310	173.7%
LEELANAU	944	1,087	143	15.1%	369	1,121	752	203.8%
LENAWEE	4,095	5,316	1,221	29.8%	4,049	6,431	2,382	58.8%
LIVINGSTON	2,364	3,221	857	36.3%	4,261	15,820	11,559	271.3%
LUCE	416	637	221	53.1%	192	139	(53)	-27.6%
MACKINAC	956	1,278	322	33.7%	190	330	140	73.7%
MACOMB	15,231	26,312	11,081	72.8%	55,569	82,357	26,788	48.2%
MANISTEE	1,495	2,332	837	56.0%	562	784	222	39.5%
MARQUETTE	4,203	5,385	1,182	28.1%	1,743	3,286	1,543	88.5%
MASON	1,672	2,559	887	53.1%	705	1,015	310	44.0%
MECOSTA	2,051	3,067	1,016	49.5%	802	1,378	576	71.8%
MENOMINEE	2,142	2,395	253	11.8%	565	952	387	68.5%
MIDLAND	2,177	4,392	2,215	101.7%	4,526	7,715	3,189	70.5%
MISSAUKEE	788	1,392	604	76.6%	141	367	226	160.3%
MONROE	4,401	6,984	2,583	58.7%	7,493	12,843	5,350	71.4%
MONTCALM	3,022	4,961	1,939	64.2%	1,152	2,236	1,084	94.1%
MONTMORENCY	769	1,243	474	61.6%	86	204	118	137.2%
MUSKEGON	8,185	12,602	4,417	54.0%	6,722	8,262	1,540	22.9%
NEWAYGO	2,285	3,788	1,503	65.8%	799	1,637	838	104.9%
OAKLAND	24,153	34,161	10,008	41.4%	99,227	150,845	51,618	52.0%
OCEANA	1,502	2,313	811	54.0%	482	850	368	76.3%
OGEMAW	1,416	2,530	1,114	78.7%	263	442	179	68.1%
ONTONAGON	675	895	220	32.6%	201	313	112	55.7%
OSCEOLA	1,329	2,237	908	68.3%	385	588	203	52.7%
OSCODA	574	1,072	498	86.8%	130	159	29	22.3%
OTSEGO	545	1,392	847	155.4%	407	876	469	115.2%
OTTAWA	4,634	6,794	2,160	46.6%	5,943	16,350	10,407	175.1%
PRESQUE ISL	1,099	1,451	352	32.0%	279	455	176	63.1%
ROSCOMMON	1,261	2,939	1,678	133.1%	377	643	266	70.6%
SAGINAW	9,521	16,867	7,346	77.2%	12,724	15,355	2,631	20.7%
ST.CLAIR	6,566	9,161	2,595	39.5%	6,269	11,715	5,446	86.9%
ST.JOSEPH	2,979	4,199	1,220	41.0%	2,198	3,389	1,191	54.2%
SANILAC	2,732	3,693	961	35.2%	1,147	1,667	520	45.3%
SCHOOLCRAFT	792	944	152	19.2%	200	296	96	48.0%
SHIAWASSEE	2,845	4,362	1,517	53.3%	3,229	4,579	1,350	41.8%
TUSCOLA	2,512	4,183	1,671	66.5%	2,020	3,373	1,353	67.0%
VAN BUREN	4,180	6,081	1,901	45.5%	2,198	3,454	1,256	57.1%
WASHTENAW	7,624	9,942	2,318	30.4%	17,969	30,066	12,097	67.3%
WAYNE	123,660	161,503	37,843	30.6%	189,878	161,689	(28,189)	-14.8%
WEXFORD	1,732	2,465	733	42.3%	483	1,174	691	143.1%

Source: Census of Population and Housing, 1970 and 1990

TABLE 1: TWENTY YEARS OF CHANGE IN FAMILY INCOME GROUPS IN MICHIGAN, 1969-1989

	NUMBER OF FAMILIES IN LOW MIDDLE INCOME GRP 1969	NUMBER OF FAMILIES MIDDLE LOW MIDDLE INCOME GRP 1989	CHANGE IN NUMBER OF FAMILIES LOW MIDDLE INCOME GRP 69-89	NUMBER OF FAMILIES MIDDLE INCOME GROUP 1969	NUMBER OF FAMILIES MIDDLE INCOME GROUP 1989	CHANGE IN NUMBER OF FAMILIES IN MIDDLE INCOME GROUP 69-89	PERCENTAGE CHANGE IN FAMILIES IN MIDDLE INCOME GROUP 69-89	NUMBER OF FAMILIES IN UPPER MIDDLE INCOME GROUP 1969	NUMBER OF FAMILIES IN UPPER MIDDLE INCOME GROUP 1989	CHANGE IN NUMBER OF FAMILIES IN UPPER MIDDLE INCOME GRP. 69-89
U.S.	10,182,551	10,694,148	511,597	10,080,214	9,788,619	(291,595)	-2.9%	7,010,098	8,847,287	1,837,189
MICHIGAN	376,332	379,629	3,297	457,807	383,718	(74,089)	-16.2%	363,177	333,962	(29,215)
ALCONA	414	677	263	296	450	154	52.0%	118	258	140
ALGER	645	560	(85)	514	487	(27)	-5.3%	186	292	106
ALLEGAN	3,947	4,697	750	4,036	4,723	687	17.0%	2,356	3,965	1,609
ALPENA	1,955	1,689	(266)	1,641	1,561	(80)	-4.9%	834	1,077	243
ANTRIM	750	1,239	489	618	924	306	49.5%	369	573	204
ARENAC	701	883	182	595	573	(22)	-3.7%	329	407	78
BARAGA	511	496	(15)	408	339	(69)	-16.9%	179	222	43
BARRY	2,122	2,659	537	2,328	2,672	344	14.8%	1,537	2,088	551
BAY	5,739	5,103	(636)	7,150	5,088	(2,062)	-28.8%	4,770	4,554	(216)
BENZIE	590	881	291	388	546	158	40.7%	214	370	156
BERRIEN	8,440	7,886	(554)	9,286	8,014	(1,272)	-13.7%	6,924	6,016	(908)
BRANCH	2,048	2,407	359	1,993	2,105	112	5.6%	1,435	1,351	(84)
CALHOUN	6,277	6,389	112	7,979	5,899	(2,080)	-26.1%	6,297	4,982	(1,315)
CASS	2,354	2,693	339	2,546	2,706	160	6.3%	1,768	1,872	104
CHARLEVOIX	974	1,351	377	808	1,203	395	48.9%	593	778	185
CHEBOYGAN	1,055	1,452	397	759	1,033	274	36.1%	467	636	169
CHIPPEWA	2,142	1,833	(309)	1,224	1,336	112	9.2%	836	919	83
CLARE	1,062	1,396	334	798	922	124	15.5%	461	625	164
CLINTON	2,213	2,596	383	2,717	2,793	76	2.8%	2,284	2,512	228
CRAWFORD	426	846	420	276	519	243	88.0%	191	371	180
DELTA	2,150	2,124	(26)	2,041	1,790	(251)	-12.3%	1,054	1,301	247
DICKINSON	1,524	1,568	44	1,431	1,235	(196)	-13.7%	680	1,092	412
EATON	2,973	3,868	895	3,837	4,269	432	11.3%	3,109	3,907	798
EMMET	1,078	1,498	420	909	1,353	444	48.8%	442	833	391
GENESEE	18,772	15,480	(3,292)	23,975	17,017	(6,958)	-29.0%	19,242	16,316	(2,926)
GLADWIN	876	1,250	374	744	891	147	19.8%	399	650	251
GOGEBIC	1,631	1,193	(438)	973	781	(192)	-19.7%	441	387	(54)
GRAND TRAVE	2,195	3,634	1,439	2,116	3,295	1,179	55.7%	1,352	2,264	912
GRATIOT	2,449	2,053	(396)	1,942	1,843	(99)	-5.1%	1,235	1,385	150
HILLSDALE	2,303	2,473	170	2,169	2,282	113	5.2%	1,241	1,540	299
HOUGHTON	2,113	1,636	(477)	1,154	1,305	151	13.1%	502	740	238
HURON	1,920	2,125	205	1,532	1,718	186	12.1%	983	1,103	120
INGHAM	10,335	9,890	(445)	12,588	10,476	(2,112)	-16.8%	10,181	9,159	(1,022)
IONIA	2,443	2,696	253	2,583	2,567	(16)	-0.6%	1,661	2,173	512
IOSCO	1,580	2,163	583	1,116	1,314	198	17.7%	556	703	147
IRON	910	865	(45)	775	583	(192)	-24.8%	343	295	(48)
ISABELLA	1,877	2,202	325	1,990	1,762	(228)	-11.5%	1,075	1,472	397
JACKSON	6,263	6,990	727	8,207	7,006	(1,201)	-14.6%	5,998	5,342	(656)
KALAMAZOO	8,648	8,417	(231)	10,309	8,885	(1,424)	-13.8%	8,243	8,132	(111)
KALKASKA	290	957	667	280	641	361	128.9%	93	369	276

Source: Census of Population and Housing, 1970 and 1990

TABLE 1: TWENTY YEARS OF CHANGE IN FAMILY INCOME GROUPS IN MICHIGAN, 1969-1989

COUNTY	NUMBER OF FAMILIES IN LOW MIDDLE INCOME GRP 1969	NUMBER OF FAMILIES IN LOW MIDDLE INCOME GRP 1989	CHANGE IN NUMBER OF FAMILIES LOW MIDDLE INCOME GRP 69-89	NUMBER OF FAMILIES MIDDLE INCOME GROUP 1969	NUMBER OF FAMILIES MIDDLE INCOME GROUP 1989	CHANGE IN NUMBER OF FAMILIES IN MIDDLE INCOME GROUP 69-89	PERCENTAGE CHANGE IN FAMILIES IN MIDDLE INCOME GROUP 69-89	NUMBER OF FAMILIES IN UPPER MIDDLE INCOME GROUP 1969	NUMBER OF FAMILIES IN UPPER MIDDLE INCOME GROUP 1989	CHANGE IN NUMBER OF FAMILIES IN UPPER MIDDLE INCOME GRP. 69-89
KENT	19,156	21,127	1,971	23,319	23,594	275	1.2%	17,259	20,548	3,289
KEWEENAW	154	90	(64)	68	70	2	2.9%	22	18	(4)
LAKE	331	490	159	226	265	39	17.3%	96	178	82
LAPEER	2,213	3,092	879	2,695	3,506	811	30.1%	2,092	2,956	864
LEELANAU	609	1,068	459	478	936	458	95.8%	417	585	168
LENAWEE	4,464	4,362	(102)	4,935	4,464	(471)	-9.5%	3,142	3,666	524
LIVINGSTON	2,256	3,495	1,239	3,153	4,361	1,208	38.3%	2,534	4,817	2,283
LUCE	299	371	72	330	211	(119)	-36.1%	188	166	(22)
MACKINAC	579	698	119	423	468	45	10.6%	203	259	56
MACOMB	17,527	26,210	8,683	31,599	30,218	(1,381)	-4.4%	33,841	31,539	(2,302)
MANISTEE	1,474	1,280	(194)	1,188	1,029	(159)	-13.4%	551	660	109
MARQUETTE	4,120	3,557	(563)	3,561	3,374	(187)	-5.3%	1,743	2,491	748
MASON	1,579	1,483	(96)	1,300	1,287	(13)	-1.0%	672	866	194
MECOSTA	1,668	1,665	(3)	1,004	1,344	340	33.9%	654	952	298
MENOMINEE	1,828	1,564	(264)	1,275	1,187	(88)	-6.9%	510	760	250
MIDLAND	2,227	3,012	785	4,005	3,035	(970)	-24.2%	2,757	2,743	(14)
MISSAUKEE	479	793	314	290	570	280	96.6%	147	308	161
MONROE	4,744	5,250	506	6,997	5,599	(1,398)	-20.0%	5,816	5,736	(80)
MONTCALM	2,628	2,881	253	2,275	2,520	245	10.8%	1,373	1,708	335
MONTMORENCY	338	643	305	181	423	242	133.7%	78	164	86
MUSKEGON	8,874	8,555	(319)	9,452	7,584	(1,868)	-19.8%	6,027	5,599	(428)
NEWAYGO	1,780	2,289	509	1,451	1,787	336	23.2%	708	1,264	556
OAKLAND	25,888	31,283	5,395	40,663	38,254	(2,409)	-5.9%	39,167	38,950	(217)
OCEANA	1,133	1,312	179	844	1,149	305	36.1%	569	655	86
OGEMAW	731	1,166	435	455	758	303	66.6%	295	481	186
ONTONAGON	829	560	(269)	605	507	(98)	-16.2%	288	276	(12)
OSCEOLA	895	1,220	325	822	977	155	18.9%	405	573	168
OSCODA	275	519	244	183	414	231	126.2%	78	152	74
OTSEGO	581	1,084	503	553	1,046	493	89.2%	355	651	296
OTTAWA	6,978	7,645	667	7,931	10,143	2,212	27.9%	5,589	9,066	3,477
PRESQUE ISL	823	963	140	621	634	13	2.1%	279	438	159
ROSCOMMON	609	1,268	659	406	822	416	102.5%	218	458	240
SAGINAW	9,280	8,568	(712)	12,352	9,195	(3,157)	-25.6%	9,247	7,721	(1,526)
ST.CLAIR	6,024	6,851	827	6,629	6,749	120	1.8%	4,651	5,542	891
ST.JOSEPH	2,708	3,218	510	2,676	3,152	476	17.8%	1,989	2,281	292
SANILAC	2,040	2,448	408	1,893	1,893	(43)	-2.2%	1,110	1,315	205
SCHOOLCRAFT	567	531	(36)	324	371	47	14.5%	265	262	(3)
SHIAWASSEE	3,100	3,389	289	3,777	3,736	(41)	-1.1%	2,794	3,106	312
TUSCOLA	2,750	3,003	253	2,623	2,541	(82)	-3.1%	1,753	2,221	468
VAN BUREN	3,342	3,846	504	2,962	3,337	375	12.7%	1,710	2,571	861
WASHTENAW	7,615	7,465	(150)	9,699	8,545	(1,154)	-11.9%	8,668	8,492	(176)
WAYNE	102,565	76,941	(25,624)	133,487	75,478	(58,009)	-43.5%	111,442	66,906	(44,536)
WEXFORD	1,256	1,559	303	1,049	1,279	230	21.9%	507	831	324

Source: Census of Population and Housing, 1970 and 1990

counties of Roscommon, Clare, Gladwin, Arenac, Manistee, and Barriga. In Livingston County, median family income rose by 28 percent, more than three times the national increase. In spite of these outliers, it must be admitted that the performance of Michigan's economy over this period has been a disappointing one and has significantly lagged behind the rest of the nation. The stagnation of Michigan's economy, however, is not the principal focus of this article: changes in the income distribution as a result of economic and social changes are the focus.

CHANGES IN INCOME DISTRIBUTION

Tables 1 and 2, detailing the breakdown of income groups for all counties in Michigan in 1969 and 1989, contain the major findings of this paper. Table 1 presents the absolute income distributions (i.e., the number of families in each income group), and the relative or percentage distribution of families in each income group appear in table 3. Policymakers who are interested in specific counties or groups of counties can focus on the regions of the state in which they are particularly interested.

In interpreting table 1, it is important to note that nationally, the number of families grew by roughly 28 percent over the twenty-year period. In Michigan, the population grew more slowly, with the number of families increasing by only about 12 percent. If the number of families in an income category increases by *less* than the overall population growth rate (28 percent nationally, 12 percent in Michigan), that category's proportionate share of the total must, of course, shrink. Similarly, growth in the number of families of an income category by a *greater* percentage than overall population growth implies an increasing proportionate population share for that income category. For example, the number of upper-income families in the U.S. grew by nearly nine million, or 84 percent, between 1969 and 1989. Since the number of families in the U.S. grew by only 28 percent, the share of high-income families *must* have grown in the U.S. This is confirmed in table 2, which shows that the proportion of high-income families grew by nearly 10 percent in the U.S. At the other extreme, the number of families of low-income status grew by nearly three million, even though median family income grew by 9 percent. However, the proportion of low-income families in the U.S. fell slightly, from 26 percent to 24.9

TABLE 2: PERCENTAGE OF FAMILIES IN INCOME GROUPS, 1969-1989

	UPPER MIDDLE INCOME 1969	UPPER MIDDLE INCOME 1989	%CHANGE UPPER MIDDLE GRP 1969-1989	UPPER INCOME 1969	UPPER INCOME 1989	CHANGE IN UPPER INCOME GRP 1969-1989
U.S.	13.7%	13.6%	-0.1%	20.7%	30.0%	9.3%
MICHIGAN	16.6%	13.6%	-3.0%	26.7%	31.6%	4.9%
ALCONA	5.8%	8.4%	2.6%	7.6%	7.5%	-0.1%
ALGER	8.7%	11.7%	3.0%	6.8%	10.0%	3.2%
ALLEGAN	14.0%	16.3%	2.3%	14.7%	23.5%	8.8%
ALPENA	11.3%	12.6%	1.4%	13.8%	16.2%	2.3%
ANTRIM	11.4%	10.9%	-0.6%	11.7%	14.1%	2.4%
ARENAC	11.5%	9.7%	-1.9%	12.1%	13.8%	1.8%
BARAGA	9.1%	10.6%	1.4%	9.2%	9.7%	0.5%
BARRY	15.7%	14.9%	-0.8%	16.2%	24.5%	8.3%
BAY	16.5%	14.9%	-1.6%	20.9%	25.4%	4.5%
BENZIE	9.8%	10.5%	0.8%	12.1%	11.5%	-0.6%
BERRIEN	16.5%	13.6%	-2.9%	19.4%	23.2%	3.8%
BRANCH	15.3%	12.2%	-3.2%	15.8%	17.7%	1.8%
CALHOUN	17.4%	13.5%	-3.9%	23.6%	25.6%	2.0%
CASS	15.7%	13.5%	-2.2%	17.9%	20.7%	2.8%
CHARLEVOIX	14.2%	12.9%	-1.4%	12.8%	16.5%	3.7%
CHEBOYGAN	11.0%	10.4%	-0.6%	11.3%	10.1%	-1.2%
CHIPPEWA	10.7%	11.3%	0.5%	8.2%	12.6%	4.5%
CLARE	10.2%	8.6%	-1.6%	10.0%	11.0%	1.1%
CLINTON	19.4%	15.7%	-3.7%	23.0%	34.7%	11.7%
CRAWFORD	11.5%	11.2%	-0.3%	13.3%	11.6%	-1.7%
DELTA	11.9%	12.7%	0.8%	13.0%	16.6%	3.6%
DICKINSON	10.9%	14.4%	3.5%	10.2%	19.8%	9.7%
EATON	17.8%	15.5%	-2.3%	27.9%	35.7%	7.8%
EMMET	10.0%	12.3%	2.3%	16.4%	19.5%	3.1%
GENESEE	17.6%	14.0%	-3.6%	27.1%	31.4%	4.3%
GLADWIN	11.0%	10.3%	-0.8%	10.2%	12.0%	1.8%
GOGEBIC	8.0%	7.9%	-0.1%	5.0%	10.1%	5.1%
GRAND TRAVER	14.2%	13.1%	-1.1%	18.1%	25.4%	7.3%
GRATIOT	12.9%	13.3%	0.4%	15.9%	17.8%	1.9%
HILLSDALE	13.2%	13.1%	-0.1%	12.9%	17.9%	5.0%
HOUGHTON	6.0%	9.1%	3.1%	7.6%	12.7%	5.2%
HURON	11.3%	11.3%	0.0%	12.0%	13.7%	1.7%
INGHAM	16.9%	14.0%	-2.8%	27.5%	32.1%	4.5%
IONIA	15.4%	15.6%	0.1%	16.2%	23.2%	7.0%
IOSCO	8.8%	8.2%	-0.7%	8.9%	10.5%	1.6%
IRON	9.1%	7.8%	-1.4%	6.0%	7.4%	1.3%
ISABELLA	12.3%	12.6%	0.4%	16.7%	20.5%	3.8%
JACKSON	17.1%	13.6%	-3.5%	23.5%	26.0%	2.6%
KALAMAZOO	17.4%	14.5%	-2.9%	25.6%	33.3%	7.7%
KALKASKA	6.7%	9.7%	3.0%	6.8%	10.9%	4.0%
KENT	17.1%	15.7%	-1.4%	22.7%	30.7%	8.0%

Source: Census of Population and Housing, 1970 and 1990

TABLE 2: PERCENTAGE OF FAMILIES IN INCOME GROUPS, 1969-1989

	UPPER MIDDLE INCOME 1969	UPPER MIDDLE INCOME 1989	%CHANGE UPPER MIDDLE GRP 1969-1989	UPPER INCOME 1969	UPPER INCOME 1989	CHANGE IN UPPER INCOME GRP 1969-1989
KEWEENAW	3.5%	3.7%	0.2%	3.3%	8.0%	4.7%
LAKE	6.4%	7.3%	0.9%	6.4%	7.4%	1.0%
LAPEER	17.7%	14.6%	-3.0%	21.0%	33.6%	12.6%
LEELANAU	14.8%	12.2%	-2.6%	13.1%	23.4%	10.3%
LENAWEE	15.2%	15.1%	-0.1%	19.6%	26.5%	7.0%
LIVINGSTON	17.4%	15.2%	-2.2%	29.2%	49.9%	20.6%
LUCE	13.2%	10.9%	-2.3%	13.5%	9.1%	-4.4%
MACKINAC	8.6%	8.5%	-0.1%	8.1%	10.9%	2.8%
MACOMB	22.0%	16.0%	-6.0%	36.1%	41.9%	5.7%
MANISTEE	10.5%	10.8%	0.4%	10.7%	12.9%	2.2%
MARQUETTE	11.3%	13.8%	2.4%	11.3%	18.2%	6.8%
MASON	11.3%	12.0%	0.7%	11.9%	14.1%	2.2%
MECOSTA	10.6%	11.3%	0.7%	13.0%	16.4%	3.4%
MENOMINEE	8.1%	11.1%	3.0%	8.9%	13.9%	4.9%
MIDLAND	17.6%	13.1%	-4.4%	28.8%	36.9%	8.1%
MISSAUKEE	8.0%	9.0%	1.0%	7.6%	10.7%	3.1%
MONROE	19.7%	15.8%	-4.0%	25.4%	35.3%	9.8%
MONTCALM	13.1%	11.9%	-1.2%	11.0%	15.6%	4.6%
MONTMORENCY	5.4%	6.1%	0.8%	5.9%	7.6%	1.7%
MUSKEGON	15.4%	13.1%	-2.2%	17.1%	19.4%	2.3%
NEWAYGO	10.1%	11.7%	1.7%	11.4%	15.2%	3.8%
OAKLAND	17.1%	13.3%	-3.8%	43.3%	51.4%	8.1%
OCEANA	12.6%	10.4%	-2.1%	10.6%	13.5%	2.9%
OGEMAW	9.3%	8.9%	-0.4%	8.3%	8.2%	-0.1%
ONTONAGON	11.1%	10.8%	-0.3%	7.7%	12.3%	4.5%
OSCEOLA	10.6%	10.2%	-0.3%	10.0%	10.5%	0.5%
OSCODA	6.3%	6.6%	0.3%	10.5%	6.9%	-3.6%
OTSEGO	14.5%	12.9%	-1.6%	16.7%	17.3%	0.7%
OTTAWA	18.0%	18.1%	0.1%	19.1%	32.7%	13.6%
PRESQUE ISLE	9.0%	11.1%	2.1%	9.0%	11.5%	2.5%
ROSCOMMON	7.6%	7.5%	-0.1%	13.1%	10.5%	-2.6%
SAGINAW	17.4%	13.4%	-4.0%	24.0%	26.6%	2.7%
ST.CLAIR	15.4%	13.8%	-1.6%	20.8%	29.3%	8.5%
ST.JOSEPH	15.8%	14.0%	-1.8%	17.5%	20.9%	3.4%
SANILAC	12.4%	11.9%	-0.4%	12.8%	15.1%	2.3%
SCHOOLCRAFT	12.3%	10.9%	-1.4%	9.3%	12.3%	3.0%
SHIAWASSEE	17.7%	16.2%	-1.5%	20.5%	23.9%	3.4%
TUSCOLA	15.0%	14.5%	-0.5%	17.3%	22.0%	4.7%
VAN BUREN	11.9%	13.3%	1.4%	15.3%	17.9%	2.6%
WASHTENAW	16.8%	13.2%	-3.6%	34.8%	46.6%	11.8%
WAYNE	16.9%	12.3%	-4.5%	28.7%	29.8%	1.1%
WEXFORD	10.1%	11.4%	1.3%	9.6%	16.1%	6.5%

Source: Census of Population and Housing, 1970 and 1990

TABLE 3: CHANGE IN FEMALE-HEADED FAMILIES, 1970-1990

	FEMALE-HEADE FAMILIES W CHILDREN 1970	PERCENTAGE OF FAMILIES W CHILDREN HEADED BY FEMALES,1970	FEMALE-HEADE FAMILIES W CHILDREN 1990	PERCENTAGE OF FAMILIES W CHILDREN HEADED BY FEMALES,1990	PERCENTAGE CHANGE IN PERCENTAGE OF FEMALE-HEADED FAMILIES WITH CHILDREN
MICHIGAN	123943	9.8%	299549	23.7%	141.2%
ALCONA	64	7.4%	195	17.3%	133.9%
ALGER	81	6.9%	186	16.3%	136.7%
ALLEGAN	624	6.4%	1940	14.7%	128.8%
ALPENA	352	7.9%	729	17.3%	120.0%
ANTRIM	121	7.1%	405	17.4%	143.9%
ARENAC	97	6.7%	378	18.8%	182.0%
BARAGA	85	8.2%	209	20.4%	148.5%
BARRY	383	7.1%	945	13.4%	90.7%
BAY	1249	7.3%	3121	20.3%	178.3%
BENZIE	87	7.9%	240	15.3%	95.1%
BERRIEN	2492	10.5%	5927	26.6%	154.1%
BRANCH	423	8.4%	1048	18.3%	117.9%
CALHOUN	2235	11.1%	4944	26.3%	135.6%
CASS	465	7.5%	1343	19.6%	160.8%
CHARLEVOIX	146	6.4%	491	16.6%	159.3%
CHEBOYGAN	199	8.6%	546	19.2%	123.8%
CHIPPEWA	433	9.6%	791	19.7%	105.0%
CLARE	204	9.2%	768	23.6%	157.3%
CLINTON	383	5.1%	1023	12.2%	138.2%
CRAWFORD	111	12.2%	296	18.2%	49.2%
DELTA	345	6.9%	883	17.0%	145.7%
DICKINSON	211	6.7%	571	15.8%	134.4%
EATON	609	5.7%	2267	16.9%	194.3%
EMMET	216	8.6%	549	15.9%	85.4%
GENESEE	7117	10.5%	20135	31.6%	202.2%
GLADWIN	115	6.3%	522	18.8%	199.3%
GOGEBIC	209	8.1%	408	19.7%	143.1%
GRAND TRAVER	453	8.5%	1527	16.9%	99.5%
GRATIOT	387	6.8%	948	17.8%	162.2%
HILLSDALE	336	6.4%	977	16.1%	151.0%
HOUGHTON	309	8.1%	617	16.5%	104.5%
HURON	313	6.7%	667	14.5%	115.9%
INGHAM	3663	10.6%	9085	25.5%	141.1%
IONIA	465	7.2%	1322	16.8%	133.4%
IOSCO	250	7.0%	648	15.7%	124.0%
IRON	129	7.5%	261	17.3%	131.9%
ISABELLA	372	7.3%	1192	18.8%	158.9%
JACKSON	1754	8.8%	4371	21.9%	149.9%
KALAMAZOO	2489	8.9%	6474	22.7%	153.8%
KALKASKA	74	10.8%	337	17.3%	60.8%
KENT	5750	9.7%	14628	20.8%	113.9%
KEWEENAW	22	9.2%	24	14.0%	51.8%
LAKE	63	10.3%	259	24.8%	139.4%
LAPEER	434	5.8%	1496	13.4%	130.9%
LEELANAU	80	5.5%	323	14.7%	168.2%
LENAWEE	842	7.2%	2161	16.8%	134.3%
LIVINGSTON	495	5.6%	1678	9.9%	77.4%
LUCE	85	11.0%	130	17.3%	57.2%
MACKINAC	104	8.0%	255	18.1%	126.0%

Source: Census of Population and Housing, 1970 and 1990

TABLE 3: CHANGE IN FEMALE-HEADED FAMILIES, 1970-1990

	FEMALE-HEADE FAMILIES W CHILDREN 1970	PERCENTAGE OF FAMILIES W CHILDREN HEADED BY FEMALES,1970	FEMALE-HEADE FAMILIES W CHILDREN 1990	PERCENTAGE OF FAMILIES W CHILDREN HEADED BY FEMALES,1990	PERCENTAGE CHANGE IN PERCENTAGE OF FEMALE-HEADED FAMILIES WITH CHILDREN
MACOMB	5913	5.9%	13997	15.1%	155.8%
MANISTEE	194	7.0%	478	17.9%	153.8%
MARQUETTE	613	7.0%	1508	15.5%	120.9%
MASON	245	8.1%	637	18.6%	130.3%
MECOSTA	215	6.7%	766	18.8%	179.5%
MENOMINEE	197	5.8%	514	15.2%	160.2%
MIDLAND	523	5.1%	1517	14.1%	177.5%
MISSAUKEE	58	6.0%	211	12.5%	108.8%
MONROE	1080	6.1%	3217	16.4%	170.8%
MONTCALM	413	7.4%	1353	18.0%	143.3%
MONTMORENCY	56	8.7%	217	20.9%	140.9%
MUSKEGON	2528	10.9%	5917	26.5%	143.4%
NEWAYGO	317	8.2%	882	16.1%	96.0%
OAKLAND	9674	7.0%	23382	16.2%	133.3%
OCEANA	162	6.6%	505	15.6%	135.6%
OGEMAW	129	8.5%	469	19.1%	126.0%
ONTONAGON	93	6.2%	150	13.4%	116.8%
OSCEOLA	153	7.5%	468	16.6%	122.5%
OSCODA	43	7.6%	133	14.8%	95.5%
OTSEGO	99	6.6%	353	13.8%	109.7%
OTTAWA	1050	5.3%	2821	10.4%	95.7%
PRESQUE ISLE	207	11.9%	244	14.5%	22.1%
ROSCOMMON	118	10.4%	431	20.2%	95.3%
SAGINAW	3105	9.5%	8945	29.4%	209.5%
ST.CLAIR	1467	8.7%	3916	18.8%	117.0%
ST.JOSEPH	543	8.1%	1598	19.1%	135.0%
SANILAC	292	5.9%	836	15.2%	158.9%
SCHOOLCRAFT	89	8.1%	187	16.7%	104.7%
SHIAWASSEE	596	6.2%	1783	17.2%	178.7%
TUSCOLA	384	5.5%	1241	15.5%	180.2%
VAN BUREN	732	9.3%	2134	20.9%	123.7%
WASHTENAW	2581	8.6%	6595	19.9%	132.4%
WAYNE	51899	14.4%	111148	38.4%	165.8%
WEXFORD	250	9.0%	756	19.8%	119.6%

Source: Census of Population and Housing, 1970 and 1990

percent. The proposition that in the U.S. there has been a "shrinking middle class" is supported by the fact that the percentage of families in the middle three groups fell from 53.3 percent to 45 percent—a reduction of over 8 percent.

The experience of Michigan has both similarities and differences with the country as a whole. In Michigan, as in the nation, the proportion of families in the upper-income group grew. However, the increase was far smaller in Michigan than it was for the nation. The share of families in the top income group grew by 4.9 percentage points in Michigan, as compared with a 9.3 percentage point increase nationwide.

At the low end of the income distribution, however, Michigan's experience is dramatically different from that of the U.S. While the proportion of low-income families fell nationally, the low-income population grew by over five percentage points in Michigan. Looking at the totals in table 2, we see that the total number of low-income families grew by over 176,000. Since the number of Michigan families grew by 268,000 over this period, it is correct to say that nearly two-thirds (176/268) of the increase in the population of Michigan families was of low-income status.

The hypothesis of the "shrinking middle class" appears to be true with a vengeance in Michigan. While the proportion of U.S. families in the middle three income categories fell between 1969 and 1989 (by eight percentage points), at least their absolute numbers grew. In the case of Michigan, not only did the proportion of families in the middle income categories fall (by ten percentage points) but their absolute number actually fell by 100,000 during a period of time when the number of families grew by 268,000.

Tables 1 and 2 describe Michigan's changing income distribution on a county by county level. Table 2 can be used to determine if the counties' middle-income categories declined at a greater rate than the overall state average. This can be done by simply adding up the middle three columns (lower-middle, middle, and upper-middle) labeled percentage changes. In 48 counties, the percentage of families in the three middle-income categories declined. Over 100,000 families disappeared from the middle class, with largest number occurring in Wayne, Genesee, Saginaw, Gratiot, and most counties in the upper peninsula.

Although a comprehensive analysis of the change in income distribution must await a full-blown econometric approach, there is one suggestive fact in common about the previously mentioned three large counties (Wayne, Genesee, and Saginaw). In all three cases, the county lost a disproportionate share of its manufacturing employment.[4] Between 1969 and 1989, the nation lost 2.6 percent and Michigan lost 18.1 percent of its manufacturing employment. Within Michigan, however, Wayne, Genesee, and Saginaw counties lost 48 percent, 39 percent, and 24 percent, respectively, of their manufacturing employment. Looking at some of the other counties that lost disproportionate shares of their middle class, a similar (but not universal) pattern emerges (Bay, Calhoun, and Manistee counties were big middle class and manufacturing employment losers). A more systematic way of analyzing the importance of manufacturing employment on income distribution is through regression analysis. By regressing the change in the proportion of families in a county in the middle-income categories on change in the share of employment in manufacturing in the county, significant findings are obtained. First, there is a statistically significant direct relationship between the change in the share of manufacturing employment in a county and the change in the proportion of families in the middle class (i.e., as the manufacturing employment declines, so does the share of families in the middle class). Second, the magnitude of this effect is large—a loss of ten percentage points of manufacturing employment results in a loss of 2.7 percentage points in middle-income membership.

Between 1969 and 1989, Michigan manufacturing employment fell by over 18 percentage points. According to our statistical analysis, this factor alone accounted for 4.85 (or 48.5 percent) of the ten percentage point reduction in middle-income membership in the state. Of course, manufacturing employment is not the *only* reason for a changing income distribution. The nation's family structure has changed in a way that has resulted in fewer middle-income families and more poverty level families than if no change in manufacturing employment had occurred.

POVERTY AND THE RISE IN FEMALE-HEADED HOUSEHOLDS

Major demographic shifts also have affected income distribution over the last twenty years, perhaps the greatest of which is the increase in the number of female-headed families (i.e., families in which there is no male parent present). Almost 60 percent of all

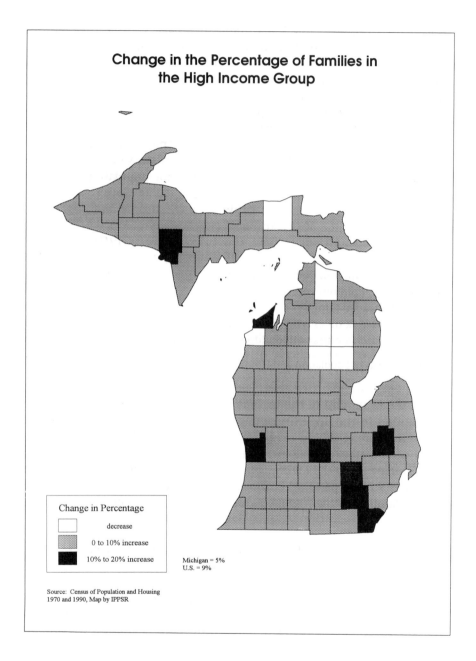

Figure 2.

that the combined forces of decreased manufacturing and blue-collar jobs, with a rise in technical-skilled jobs, and the movement of jobs from central cities to suburban fringes have increased the unemployment of urban workers, primarily black males. With the rising number of out-of-the-labor-force men, there has been a reduction in marriageable mates for black women, leading to increased female-headed units, and decreased husband-wife households.

Most affected by changes in family income are families headed by persons younger than 30. In "Vanishing Dreams: The Economic Plight of America's Young Families" published by the Children's Defense Fund, analysis shows that the median income of young families in 1990 was nearly one-third or 32 percent below the median for such families in 1973. In spite of periods of sharp economic growth in the U.S. during the 1980s, young families saw their median income continue to fall. The change in the income levels of families, and young families in particular, is the major cause of Michigan's increasing child poverty. "More than half of the increase in the number of poor children in American since 1973 has been the result of falling incomes and rising poverty among young families."[5] The consequences of falling incomes and rising poverty for young families are severe. Meeting children's basic needs of food and shelter is problematic for increasing numbers of families and children among the homeless population in Michigan. Many do not have health insurance, health care, or safe child care. In a 1990 study of child deaths in Michigan, the Michigan Department of Public Health showed that poor children are two and one-half times more likely to die than nonpoor children and that they experience this higher death rate regardless of race, ethnic background, age, gender, or place of residence. While four out of five nonpoor children went to a physician's office for routine preventive care, only 52 percent of poor children received similar care. Forty-eight percent of poor children relied on hospital or community clinics or had no regular source of care.

Although the purpose of this article is measurement of changes in Michigan's income distribution, some policy recommendations are cautiously offered.

Single-parent families are more likely to be in poverty because of increased needs and reduced income sources. In fact, all children have two parents—it is the withdrawal of assistance by one parent that renders the children and custodial parent at risk. Increasing the use of the Child Support Enforcement Program assists in establishing paternity and obtaining child support payments from absent parents of both Aid to Families with Dependent Children and non-AFDC children. Genetic tests can be paid for by the federal government to identify absent fathers. Working with employers or the Department of Treasury to withhold wages from fathers who are delinquent in their child support and collaborating with other states to develop a federal tracking system would increase the income of some of the poorest families.

A failure of our nation's welfare system is that continued eligibility for assistance discourages work effort and earning. What is needed are policies that condition assistance (including child care assistance) with work effort, e.g., expansion of the earned income tax credit, wage rate subsidies for low-skilled workers, and employer-based marginal employment subsidies for employers who add to their work force.

The inability of young men with high school educations to find high-paying jobs coupled with the loss of jobs in the state's inner-city neighborhoods has reduced the ability of young men to be able to support a family. Improving the job opportunities for young men would give them incentives to continue their education and to form stable family relationships.

One of the most effective disease prevention devices is childhood immunizations. An investment of $1 in childhood immunizations saves as much as $10 in short-term health costs. Although all children are vaccinated before entering kindergarten, it is estimated that less than 60 percent of the state's children are fully immunized by age two. Other prevention programs for children, including the Early and Periodic Screening Diagnosis and Treatment Program, childhood injury prevention programs, and lead screening programs, have all demonstrated success and cost-effectiveness. Continued expansion of these programs by the state will ensure that children enter school healthy and physically ready to learn.

The issue of targeting of income transfer dollars must be confronted. Since a majority of low-income families are young and have children, a redirection of income transfer policies toward children (and investment) and away from the elderly (and consumption) can be tried. If Social Security and Medicare used means-testing and income to determine eligibility, more funds could be targeted to younger families.

Optimal tax theory teaches us that the progressivity of tax systems should depend on the inequality of the underlying income distribution. A change toward increased inequality would imply increased use of mildly *progressive* tax instruments like Michigan's income tax and decreased use of mildly *regressive* instruments like Michigan's sales tax. Changes in the income tax to raise the personal exemption for young children would have the effect of giving additional income when the need for child care, housing, and food is most critical.

Studies show that a correlate of the national trend to inequality is a widening of the wage gap between high school and college graduate jobs. Consequently, expanding the proportion of Michigan's workforce that consists of college graduates would *both* increase median earnings and reduce inequality.

CONCLUSION

Viewing the state as a whole, the twenty-year period between the 1970 and the 1990 census has not been good for the Michigan economy, at least as measured by family income. While median real-family income rose by 9 percent in the U.S., it has actually fallen by 1.4 percent in Michigan. Michigan was once significantly richer than the rest of the nation—with a median family income 15 percent above the U.S. median—but now over 70 percent of this advantage is gone. The stagnation of Michigan's economy is, however, by no means uniform with a number of counties enjoying double digit increases in real income, offset by others with double digit decreases.

During the twenty-year period of our analysis, the U.S. income distribution has become more unequal, with the middle-income groups losing membership to the richest and poorest categories. This trend, with one caveat, has appeared with a vengeance in Michigan. While Michigan has experienced a greater shrinkage of the middle-income category, the state has *not* had the growth in membership at the top end that the nation has had. Consequently, Michigan has outstripped the nation in its disproportionate growth in the number of low-income families. Although it is hazardous to make causal inferences without a full-scale econometric analysis, county by county income distribution data do reveal two statistically significant causes for the increased inequality in Michigan's income distribution. First, the loss of manufacturing has contributed to the increase in income inequality. Indeed, the state's loss of manufacturing employment was far greater, in proportion, than the nation's, and consequently its move toward more inequality was more severe than nationwide. Second, the rise in female-headed families in Michigan has significantly contributed to the increase in families at the lower end of the income scale.[6]

NOTES

1. See *The Economic Report of the President* (Washington D.C.: U.S. Government Printing Office, 1994).
2. There are a large number of studies both documenting and attempting to explain this trend, see the special issue of the *Quarterly Journal of Economics* (February 1992).
3. H. Brazer, *Michigan's Fiscal and Economic Structure* (Ann Arbor: University of Michigan Press, 1982).
4. Data from the Bureau of the Census, the Bureau of Economic Analysis, and the Michigan Department of Public Health were obtained from the Michigan Databases at the Institute for Public Policy and Social Research, Michigan State University.
5. "Vanishing Dreams: The Economic Plight of America's Young Families," Children's Defense Fund and Northeastern University's Center for Labor Market Studies, 1992.
6. Partial support for this paper was provided by the Kids Count grant from the Annie Casey Foundation.

Families' Poverty in Labor Market Areas in Michigan

Janet L. Bokemeier and Jean Kayitsinga

Level of poverty is a direct indicator of quality of life. Changing economic climate is an important factor in the rise of poverty in non-metropolitan, or rural, labor markets. But poverty cannot be understood without making reference to the significant and continuing changes in family structure. Using data from the 1980 and 1990 population census, we examine poverty rates for individuals and families with different ages, race, employment status, and education in non-metropolitan, metropolitan, and mixed labor market areas.

We are particularly interested in non-metropolitan areas because recent studies report greater vulnerability among non-metropolitan populations to poverty, unemployment, and underemployment.[1] The common image of poverty is of inner-city African-Americans, unemployed and living in neighborhood ghettos.[2] One reason for this perception is that more people—and consequently more poor people—live in metropolitan areas. In Michigan about 80 percent of the state's residents live in metropolitan counties and 20 percent live in the other sixty-one counties that are classified as non-metropolitan.

However, people living in non-metropolitan areas, especially children, have as high or higher rates of poverty as those in metropolitan areas. Persons at higher risk of poverty, such as African-Americans or

45

line of reasoning, family characteristics such as marital status and number of children also act in a way that disadvantages workers, especially women, by limiting skills enhancement and labor attachment. Increasing rates of female employment, higher levels of educational attainment, and decreasing family size should result in improved economic status of families.

However, studies that try to explain changing poverty rates by studying female employment, educational attainment, and number of children find these variables are not adequate to explain changing poverty.[9] Rather, social scientists find that when comparing metropolitan and non-metropolitan people in terms of unemployment, underemployment and child poverty rates, families in non-metropolitan areas are disadvantaged in ways that are not accounted for by these individual level factors. In terms of children's poverty rates, the changing family structure with a greater incidence of female-headed households is as important a factor in accounting for children's vulnerability to economic distress as the structure of economic opportunity and labor market characteristics.

MICHIGAN LABOR MARKET AREAS

A labor market is a set of relationships between buyers and sellers of labor, including such phenomena as exchanges of labor and wages between employers and workers. Implied in the notion of labor markets is the idea that these exchanges and relationships occur in a particular locale, what we call a labor market area. Thus, a labor market area (LMA) represents the geographical arena in which people seek work and employers find workers. A majority of the workers will both live and work in the area.

Various geographical delineations (such as standard metropolitan statistical areas, counties, states or regions) have been used to represent labor market areas. One shortcoming of these areas is that it is difficult to determine non-metropolitan labor markets in which individual-record census data can be studied. To help study non-metropolitan labor markets, a regional research group sponsored by the Economic Research Service, Agricultural and Non-metropolitan Economic Division of the United States Department of Agriculture met and identified LMAs using a five percent Public Use Micro data Sample D (PUMS-D) of 1980 census on commuting patterns of

American workers. Labor market areas are groups of counties that encompass the county of residence and the county of work.[10]

People often cross state lines to work, so this designation of LMAs does not limit consideration to counties within specific state boundaries or necessarily center on metropolitan areas. The attractive aspect of the LMA is its conceptualization as a region that encompasses both the place of residence and the place of work of a local population.

Why use an LMA and not another unit of analysis? First, these areas are designated on the basis of actual labor market activity rather than for other purposes such as governance in the case of counties or states. Second, we did not want to look at individual counties because they vary in size and people often cross county boundaries to commute to work. Because some workers cross state lines in commuting to work, we have not restricted LMAs by state boundaries either. This county group approach can overcome problems with single counties and include non-metropolitan areas, but it still depends on conceptual criteria to construct groupings.

For Michigan, this analysis grouped counties into thirteen LMAs, which can be classified as either metropolitan or non-metropolitan[11] based on county classifications. We have added a category, mixed LMAs, to represent labor market areas with a substantial population in both metropolitan and non-metropolitan areas.

Two out of thirteen LMAs in Michigan (Detroit and Lansing) are characterized as metropolitan. Six are considered mixed because they include both metropolitan and non-metropolitan counties. Those LMAs considered mixed are the Saginaw, Grand Rapids, Kalamazoo, Jackson, Monroe, and Berrien areas. The remaining five LMAs in Michigan—Oscoda, Antrim, Wexford, Marquette, and Forest—are considered non-metropolitan (see figure 1).

This analysis will be limited to those LMAs wholly composed of Michigan counties. Because this will result in excluding five counties, the data presented here will not coincide with state statistics. To help avoid confusion, we have included state-level statistics. First, this article will analyze poverty rates for non-metropolitan, metropolitan, and mixed LMAs in 1980 and 1990. Second, we will compare poverty rates in married-couple families, families headed by a female without a husband, families of different races, and families of different ages. Third, we will examine the employment and educational attainment levels in different types of LMAs in order to see if these factors are associated with differences in poverty between LMAs. Finally, we will

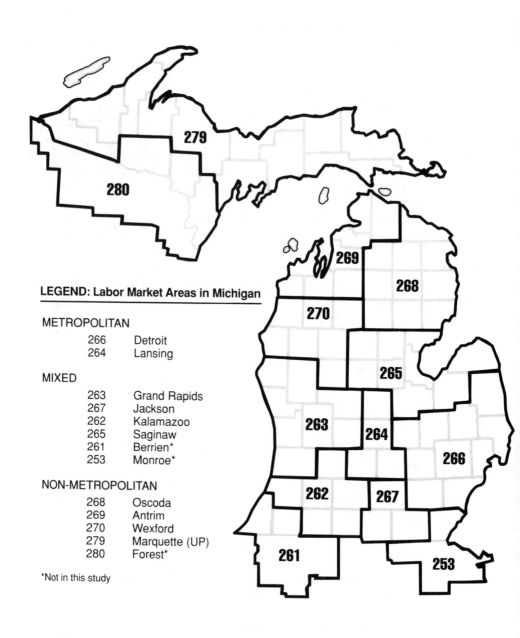

LEGEND: Labor Market Areas in Michigan

METROPOLITAN

    266   Detroit
    264   Lansing

MIXED

    263   Grand Rapids
    267   Jackson
    262   Kalamazoo
    265   Saginaw
    261   Berrien*
    253   Monroe*

NON-METROPOLITAN

    268   Oscoda
    269   Antrim
    270   Wexford
    279   Marquette (UP)
    280   Forest*

*Not in this study

Figure 1.

use methods of direct standardization to adjust poverty rates by employment rates and family size using 1980 as our base year. This shows whether changes in the poverty rate are associated with changes in family structure, employment levels, or family size.

Poverty in Michigan LMAs. An indicator of the economic status of a particular place is the poverty rate. The poverty rate was determined both in the 1980 and 1990 censuses by classifying families and unrelated individuals as above or below the poverty level by comparing their previous year's income to an income cutoff or poverty threshold that varies by family size, number of children, and age of the family householder. This threshold is computed on a national basis only and is not adjusted for regional, state, or local variations in the cost of living.

We will describe poverty by comparing: (1) personal poverty rates, or the percentage of individual residents of all ages who have incomes below the poverty thresholds; (2) per capita income, or the mean income computed from every man, woman, and child in a particular group and distribution of family income; and (3) family poverty rates, or the percentage of individuals who live in households with family incomes below the poverty threshold. The personal poverty rate is the most widely used indicator of poverty.[12] This indicator does not, however, reflect changes in the distribution of income below the poverty threshold.[13]. The second approach for comparing the economic wealth of Michigan families is to analyze the distribution of income and per capita income. Finally we will describe family poverty rates.

Because the Michigan population is much larger in metropolitan areas, the actual number of poor people is higher in metropolitan LMAs. However, we find that people in non-metropolitan LMAs are more likely to be poor—that is, they have higher rates of poverty.

Changes in Personal Poverty by LMAs, 1980-1990. Table 1 shows the official poverty rates of Michigan and the Michigan LMAs in 1980 and 1990. In 1980, 9.5 percent of Michigan residents had incomes below the official poverty level. By 1990 the personal poverty rate in Michigan had increased to 13.1 percent (i.e., a 38.7 percent increase over ten years). About one of every eight persons in Michigan had an income less than the poverty level.

In non-metropolitan LMAs in 1980, 11.2 percent of people had incomes below the poverty level. This non-metropolitan rate is much higher than for those living in mixed and metropolitan LMAs. At the end of the decade the non-metropolitan poverty rate (14.9 percent)

Labor market areas	Total persons in poverty in 1980	Total persons for whom poverty was determined in 1980	Personal poverty rate in 1980	Total persons in poverty in 1990	Total persons for whom poverty was determined in 1990	Personal poverty rate in 1990	% of change
(1)	(2)	(3)	(4)	(5)	(6)	(7)	(8)
Metropolitan	567754	6104587	9.30%	719413	5439481	13.20%	42.20%
Detroit	521265	5622231	9.30%	661099	4992293	13.20%	42.80%
Lansing	46489	482356	9.60%	58314	447188	13.00%	35.30%
Mixed	245053	2647431	9.30%	313232	2498791	12.50%	35.40%
Kalamazoo	58518	603329	9.70%	74669	560412	13.30%	37.40%
Grand Rapids	90590	1064450	8.50%	111240	1076824	10.30%	21.40%
Saginaw	70756	682606	10.40%	95942	591362	16.20%	56.50%
Jackson	25189	297046	8.50%	31381	270193	11.60%	37.00%
Non-Metropolitan	88975	791996	11.20%	109570	735300	14.90%	32.60%
Oscoda	20751	173943	11.90%	25755	166840	15.40%	29.40%
Antrim	17691	184930	9.60%	20258	189562	10.70%	11.70%
Wexford	20337	161566	12.60%	27195	145025	18.80%	49.00%
Marquette	30196	271557	11.10%	36362	233873	15.50%	39.80%
Michigan	945874	10003283	9.50%	1190698	9077016	13.10%	38.70%

TABLE 1: CHANGES IN PERSONAL POVERTY BY LABOR MARKET AREAS, 1980-1990

Source: Population Censuses, 1980 and 1990

Note: Columns 3 and 6 show the total persons for whom poverty was determined respectively in 1980 and 1990. Persons for whom poverty was determined include all persons except institutionalized persons, persons in military group quarters and in college dormitories, and unrelated individuals under 15 years old (U.S. Bureau of the Census). Columns 4 and 7 display respectively the personal poverty rate in 1980 and 1990. The personal poverty rate is computed as the total number of persons in poverty divided by the total number of persons for whom poverty status was determined. The percentage of change in column 8 is computed as the percentage of the difference between column 7 and column 4 divided by column 4.

TABLE 2:   FAMILY INCOME BY LABOR MARKET AREAS IN 1979

Income	Metro Number	%	Mixed Number	%	Non-Metro Number	%	Michigan Total	%	Cumulative %
(1)	(2)	(3)	(4)	(5)	(6)	(7)	(8)	(9)	(10)
Less than $5,000	86709	6.0%	38215	5.9%	14434	7.4%	146435	6.1%	6.1%
$5,000-$9,999	143652	9.9%	81005	12.5%	38693	19.9%	279247	11.6%	17.7%
$10,000-$14,999	149746	10.3%	88851	13.8%	36419	18.8%	291250	12.1%	29.8%
$15,000-$24,999	373600	25.7%	205244	31.8%	61174	31.5%	675716	28.1%	57.9%
$25,000-$34,999	335685	23.1%	135893	21.0%	28509	14.7%	523599	21.8%	79.7%
$35,000-$49,999	241589	16.7%	68449	10.6%	10758	5.5%	332258	13.8%	93.5%
$50,000-$74,999	90559	6.2%	20868	3.2%	3010	1.6%	117452	4.9%	98.4%
$75,000 and more	29739	2.0%	7110	1.1%	1121	0.6%	38953	1.6%	100.0%
TOTAL	1451479	100.0%	645635	100.0%	194118	100.0%	2404910	100.0%	
Per capita income*	$20,594		$18,398		$15,520		$17,302		

FAMILY INCOME BY LABOR MARKET AREAS IN 1989

Income	Metro Number	%	Mixed Number	%	Non-Metro Number	%	Michigan Total	%	Cumulative %
(1)	(2)	(3)	(4)	(5)	(6)	(7)	(8)	(9)	(10)
Less than $5,000	62590	4.3%	23197	3.4%	7343	3.2%	96277	3.9%	3.9%
$5,000-$9,999	82750	5.7%	41596	6.1%	19005	8.2%	148957	6.1%	10.0%
$10,000-$14,999	79018	5.4%	49471	7.2%	26292	11.4%	160980	6.5%	16.5%
$15,000-$24,999	185409	12.8%	115467	16.8%	54471	23.6%	369259	15.0%	31.5%
$25,000-$34,999	203302	14.0%	122462	17.9%	46141	20.0%	387209	15.7%	47.3%
$35,000-$49,999	300364	20.7%	155551	22.7%	43629	18.9%	519584	21.1%	68.4%
$50,000-$74,999	325952	22.4%	122814	17.9%	24721	10.7%	491146	20.0%	88.4%
$75,000 and more	213607	14.7%	54806	8.0%	9194	4.0%	285069	11.6%	100.0%
TOTAL	1452992	100.0%	685364	100.0%	230796	100.0%	2458481	100.0%	
Per capita income*	$27,694		$23,549		$15,520		$22,922		

Source: Population Censuses, 1980 and 1990.
* The per capita income is adjusted for inflation.

again was higher than the metropolitan (13.2 percent) and mixed LMA poverty rates (12.5 percent).

Among Michigan LMAs, the highest personal poverty rates in 1990 were in the non-metropolitan LMAs, with the Wexford (18.8 percent), Marquette (15.5 percent) and Oscoda (15.4 percent) non-metropolitan LMAs reporting the highest percentages.

In general the LMAs with the lowest poverty levels are the mixed LMAs. The lowest level of poverty in 1990 was in the Grand Rapids LMA (10.3 percent). However, the poverty rates do vary among non-metropolitan and mixed LMAs. While most mixed LMAs show low levels, the Saginaw LMA has a very high poverty rate, with about one of every six people living in poverty. While most non-metropolitan LMAs have higher poverty rates, Antrim LMA has the second-lowest percentage of people below the poverty level, with 10.7 percent of its population below poverty in 1990.

In general, the personal poverty rate increased by a greater proportion in metropolitan LMAs than elsewhere. For example, in the Detroit LMA, the personal poverty rate rose sharply, increasing from 9.3 percent to 13.2 percent. Again, some areas have experienced greater changes in poverty rates than others. Among non-metropolitan LMAs, the changes in poverty rate over the decade varied widely, from a low of only 11.7 percent in the Antrim area to a high of 49 percent in Wexford LMA.

Per Capita Income and Distribution of Family Income. Another approach for comparing economic status of Michigan families is to contrast per capita income reported by people within LMAs. These figures are reported in table 2. For Michigan, the per capita income in 1980 was $17,302, and it increased to $22,922 by 1989. (These figures are adjusted for inflation and reported in 1979 dollar values.) The per capita income in non-metropolitan LMAs is consistently the lowest. The non-metropolitan LMAs' average per capita income has not increased over the past ten years, as did per capita income in metropolitan and mixed LMAs. This suggests that non-metropolitan LMAs lack the more wealthy economic base for provision of resources and services to the needy.

In 1979 and 1989 the family incomes in non-metropolitan LMAs were substantially less than in metropolitan and mixed LMAs. In 1989, 10 percent of Michigan families had incomes less than $10,000 and 31.6 percent had incomes over $50,000. In non-metropolitan LMAs 11.4 percent had incomes less than $10,000 and only 14.7 percent had

TABLE 3: CHANGES IN FAMILY POVERTY BY LABOR MARKET AREAS, 1980-1990

Labor market areas	Total families in 1980	Total families in poverty in 1980	% of families in poverty in 1980	Total families in 1990	Total families in poverty in 1990	% of families in poverty in 1990	% change in poverty rate
(1)	(2)	(3)	(4)	(5)	(6)	(7)	(8)
Metropolitan	**1451479**	**118644**	**8.2%**	**1452992**	**151954**	**10.5%**	**27.9%**
Detroit	1339407	110484	8.2%	1336148	141505	10.6%	28.4%
Lansing	112072	8160	7.3%	116844	10449	8.9%	22.8%
Mixed	**645635**	**51233**	**7.9%**	**685364**	**66098**	**9.6%**	**21.5%**
Kalamazoo	147077	11928	8.1%	153600	15060	9.8%	20.9%
Grand Rapids	261586	19020	7.3%	292824	23165	7.9%	8.8%
Saginaw	162733	14888	9.1%	163691	21104	12.9%	40.9%
Jackson	74239	5397	7.3%	75249	6769	9.0%	23.7%
Non-Metropolitan	**194118**	**18670**	**9.6%**	**207182**	**22952**	**11.1%**	**15.2%**
Oscoda	43943	4945	11.3%	49042	5878	12.0%	6.5%
Antrim	45884	3785	8.2%	53558	4282	8.0%	-3.1%
Wexford	38951	4066	10.4%	40484	5519	13.6%	30.6%
Marquette	65340	5874	9.0%	64098	7273	11.3%	26.2%
Michigan	**2404910**	**198391**	**8.2%**	**2458481**	**251687**	**10.2%**	**24.1%**

Source: Population Censuses, 1980 and 1990

Note: Columns 4 and 7 show the family poverty rate in 1980 and in 1990 respectively. The family poverty rate is computed as the number of families in poverty divided by the total number of families. The percentage of change in column 8 is computed as the difference between column 7 and column 4 divided by column 4.

incomes over $50,000. (These income data have not been adjusted for inflation.)

Families' Poverty. Another approach to describe poverty is to examine the percentage of families who report income levels below the poverty threshold (see table 3). Poverty thresholds are based on family incomes and adjusted for family size and age. In 1990 one of every ten Michigan families had incomes less than poverty level. As with personal poverty and per capita income, the non-metropolitan LMAs have higher rates of family poverty than metropolitan and mixed LMAs. Over time, this difference is decreasing as the rate of change is greatest in metropolitan LMAs.

Among non-metropolitan LMAs there is considerable difference in the rate of family poverty and changes in percentage of families living below poverty. In the Antrim LMA, the poverty rate is the lowest, and over the past decade it declined by a fraction of a percent. In contrast, the Wexford LMA has the highest family poverty rate in Michigan and it sharply increased from 1980 to 1990.

Within the Detroit LMA there is considerable difference among counties in terms of poverty. For example, Oakland County had a family poverty rate of 4.4 percent in 1990, in contrast to Wayne County's poverty rate of 16.9 percent in 1990. These changes reflect the changing economic vitality of the LMA as well as residential mobility and business relocations within the LMA. The family incomes and family poverty rates significantly vary across non-metropolitan LMAs as well. For example, in the Oscoda LMA the county family poverty rates range from a low of 7.1 percent in Otsego to a high of 17.7 percent in Ogemaw County. The highest county family poverty rate in Michigan is found in non-metropolitan Lake County (20.2 percent). The tradeoff in our analyses is that we mask these intra-LMA phenomena and highlight the multi-county area economic and demographic characteristics.

MICHIGAN FAMILIES IN POVERTY

Female-Headed Households' Poverty. In 1990 the number of Michigan households headed by women had increased to 12.9 percent. The proportion of female households is higher in metropolitan LMAs (14.6 percent) than in non-metropolitan LMAs (8.7 percent) and mixed LMAs (11.0 percent).[14] In Michigan female-headed households are

TABLE 4: CHANGES IN FEMALE FAMILY HOUSEHOLDS' POVERTY BY LABOR MARKET AREAS, 1980-1990

Labor market areas	Total female-headed households in 1980	Total female-headed households in poverty in 1980	% of female-headed households in poverty in 1980	Total female-headed households in 1990	Total female-headed households in poverty in 1990	% of female-headed households in poverty in 1990	% of change
(1)	(2)	(3)	(4)	(5)	(6)	(7)	(8)
Metropolitan	241040	73219	30.4%	293445	103630	35.3%	16.3%
Detroit	226426	69351	30.6%	275311	97846	35.5%	16.0%
Lansing	14614	3868	26.5%	18134	5784	31.9%	20.5%
Mixed	78522	24299	30.9%	99164	36314	36.6%	18.3%
Kalamazoo	18523	5781	31.2%	23624	8529	36.1%	15.7%
Grand Rapids	31530	9315	29.5%	40103	12995	32.4%	9.7%
Saginaw	19972	6846	34.3%	24976	11276	45.1%	31.7%
Jackson	8497	2357	27.7%	10461	3514	33.6%	21.1%
Non-Metropolitan	18374	5753	31.3%	24193	9057	37.4%	19.6%
Oscoda	3860	1320	34.2%	5208	2144	41.2%	20.4%
Antrim	4371	1181	27.0%	6246	1743	27.9%	3.3%
Wexford	3757	1240	33.0%	4914	2212	45.0%	36.4%
Marquette	6386	2012	31.5%	7825	2958	37.8%	20.0%
Michigan	352256	108089	30.7%	433466	155142	35.8%	16.6%

Source: Population Censuses, 1980 and 1990

Note: Columns 4 and 7 represent respectively the poverty rate in 1980 and 1990 for female-headed households. The poverty rate for female-headed households is computed as the number of female-headed households in poverty divided by the total number of female-headed households. The percentage of change in column 8 is computed as the difference between column 7 and column 4 divided by column 4.

Labor market areas	Families with children less than 18 in 1980	Families with children less than 18 in poverty in 1980	% families with children less than 18 in poverty in 1980	Families with children less than 18 in 1990	Families with children less than 18 in poverty in 1990	% families with children less than 18 in poverty in 1990	%change in poverty rate
(1)	(2)	(3)	(4)	(5)	(6)	(7)	(8)
Metropolitan	821441	96912	11.8%	759852	126122	16.6%	40.7%
Detroit	756885	90513	12.0%	696406	117454	16.9%	41.0%
Lansing	64556	6399	9.9%	63446	8668	13.7%	37.8%
Mixed	363405	39925	11.0%	363230	53634	14.8%	34.4%
Kalamazoo	80544	9406	11.7%	79848	12303	15.4%	31.9%
Grand Rapids	148347	14990	10.1%	159439	19024	11.9%	18.1%
Saginaw	93361	11409	12.2%	84579	16923	20.0%	63.7%
Jackson	41153	4120	10.0%	39364	5384	13.7%	36.6%
Non-Metropolitan	101614	12582	12.4%	100173	16647	16.6%	34.2%
Oscoda	22260	3075	13.8%	22066	3991	18.1%	30.9%
Antrim	24531	2549	10.4%	26772	3180	11.9%	14.3%
Wexford	20108	2800	13.9%	19717	4141	21.0%	50.8%
Marquette	34715	4158	12.0%	31618	5335	16.9%	40.9%
Michigan	1350264	157054	11.6%	1281108	204821	16.0%	37.5%

TABLE 5: CHANGES IN POVERTY FOR FAMILIES WITH CHILDREN LESS THAN 18 YEARS OLD, 1980-1990

Source: Population Censuses, 1980 and 1990

almost twice as likely to be in poverty as other family households, with about one out of every three female-headed households reporting incomes at or below poverty. The poverty rate of families with female householders has increased throughout the state over the past decade (see table 4). As with family poverty rates, the non-metropolitan female householders are slightly more likely to live in poverty than those in metropolitan or mixed LMAs. Thus, although non-metropolitan families have the lowest proportion of families headed by females, these non-metropolitan female householders have the highest rates of poverty.

Poverty Rates For Families with Children. The poverty rate for families with children is considerably higher than for all Michigan families, and the rate of increase in poverty over the past decade has been greater among families with children (see table 5). In 1990 one of every six Michigan families with children in non-metropolitan and metropolitan LMAs reported incomes less than the poverty threshold. Mixed LMA families with children had a slightly lower poverty rate of 14.8 percent. Among the non-metropolitan LMAs the poverty rates widely vary from a low of 11.9 percent in the Antrim LMA to a high of 21.0 percent in the Wexford LMA.

The poverty rate for families with female householders in which children below eighteen years of age are living is substantially higher than the poverty rates in all other families with children below eighteen years of age (see table 6). By 1990 nearly one of every two Michigan female-headed households with children present was in poverty. The highest poverty rates were reported in the Saginaw mixed LMA and in Wexford LMA with 57.7 percent and 57.4 percent in poverty. The differences in poverty rate of female householders with children are only slight. Across all LMAs the poverty rate for families with children and a female householder has increased substantially over the past decade.

An increasing proportion of Michigan children will spend part of their childhood in a home with a female householder. Increasingly, Michigan children are highly likely to spend part of their childhood in poverty as well.

Poverty Rates by Age. In Michigan the number of elderly residents has significantly increased over the past decade. However, this change has not been the same in all areas of the state. The proportion of Michigan elderly persons who live in non-metropolitan LMAs has increased in the past ten years, while the proportion in mixed LMAs

TABLE 6: CHANGES IN POVERTY FOR FEMALE-HEADED FAMILIES WITH CHILDREN LESS THAN 18 YEARS OLD, 1980-1990

Labor market areas	Female-headed households with children less than 18 in 1980	Female-headed households with children less than 18 in poverty in 1980	Poverty rate for female-headed households with children less than 18 in 1980	Female-headed households with children less than 18 in 1990	Female-headed households with children less than 18 in poverty in 1990	Poverty rate for female-headed households with children less than 18 in 1990	% change in poverty rate
(1)	(2)	(3)	(4)	(5)	(6)	(7)	(8)
Metropolitan	171378	68008	39.7%	196489	94284	48.0%	20.9%
Detroit	160424	64286	40.1%	183566	88918	48.4%	20.9%
Lansing	10954	3722	34.0%	12923	5366	41.5%	22.2%
Mixed	57275	22787	39.8%	70460	33616	47.7%	19.9%
Kalamazoo	13752	5491	39.9%	17090	7871	46.1%	15.3%
Grand Rapids	23044	8787	38.1%	28178	12168	43.2%	13.2%
Saginaw	14537	6332	43.6%	17953	10357	57.7%	32.4%
Jackson	5942	2177	36.6%	7239	3220	44.5%	21.4%
Non-Metropolitan	12297	5114	41.6%	16416	8162	49.7%	19.6%
Oscoda	2747	1176	42.8%	3510	1859	53.0%	23.7%
Antrim	2985	1059	35.5%	4259	1647	38.7%	9.0%
Wexford	2603	1102	42.3%	3550	2037	57.4%	35.5%
Marquette	3962	1777	44.9%	5097	2619	51.4%	14.6%
Michigan	251300	100387	39.9%	294950	141744	48.1%	20.3%

Source: Population Censuses, 1980 and 1990

TABLE 7: CHANGES IN POVERTY FOR THE ELDERLY BY LABOR MARKET AREAS, 1980-1990							
Labor market areas	Persons 65+ in poverty in 1980	Total persons 65+ for whom poverty was determined in 1980	Poverty rate for persons 65+ in 1980	Persons 65+ in poverty in 1990	Total persons 65+ for whom poverty was determined in 1990	Poverty rate for persons 65+ in 1990	% of change
(1)	(2)	(3)	(4)	(5)	(6)	(7)	(8)
Metropolitan	54251	488348	11.10%	62134	600966	10.30%	-6.90%
Detroit	50429	454251	11.10%	58045	558968	10.40%	-6.50%
Lansing	3822	34097	11.20%	4089	41998	9.70%	-13.10%
Mixed	28868	236580	12.20%	30260	287159	10.50%	-13.60%
Kalamazoo	6195	55245	11.20%	6530	65555	10.00%	-11.20%
Grand Rapids	11149	95132	11.70%	11319	115249	9.80%	-16.20%
Saginaw	8222	58388	14.10%	8802	72855	12.10%	-14.20%
Jackson	3302	27815	11.90%	3609	33500	10.80%	-9.30%
Non-Metropolitan	15320	92374	16.60%	15261	113645	13.40%	-19.00%
Oscoda	3761	21948	17.10%	3999	29273	13.70%	-20.30%
Antrim	3312	20053	16.50%	2955	26463	11.20%	-32.40%
Wexford	3130	18750	16.70%	3096	21664	14.30%	-14.40%
Marquette	5117	31623	16.20%	5211	36245	14.40%	-11.10%
Michigan	104738	861373	12.20%	114086	1054564	10.80%	-11.00%

Source: Population Censuses, 1980 and 1990

	Total persons < 18	Persons < 18 in poverty	Poverty rate persons < 18	Total persons 18-64	Persons 18-64 in poverty	Poverty rate persons 18-64	Total persons 65+	Persons 65 + in poverty	Poverty rate persons 65 +	Total persons for whom poverty was deter-mined	Total persons in poverty	Total persons poverty rate
(1)	(2)	(3)	(4)	(5)	(6)	(7)	(8)	(9)	(10)	(11)	(12)	(13)
Metropolitan	**1420672**	**276449**	**19.50%**	**3417843**	**380830**	**11.10%**	**600966**	**62134**	**10.30%**	**5439481**	**719413**	**13.20%**
Detroit	1300999	258203	19.80%	3132326	344851	11.00%	558968	58045	10.40%	4992293	661099	13.20%
Lansing	119673	18246	15.20%	285517	35979	12.60%	41998	4089	9.70%	447188	58314	13.00%
Mixed	**701027**	**118340**	**16.90%**	**1510605**	**164632**	**10.90%**	**287159**	**30260**	**10.50%**	**2498791**	**313232**	**12.50%**
Kalamazoo	151078	27214	18.00%	343779	40925	11.90%	65555	6530	10.00%	560412	74669	13.30%
Grand Rapids	313701	43390	13.80%	647874	56531	8.70%	115249	11319	9.80%	1076824	111240	10.30%
Saginaw	161092	35732	22.20%	357415	51408	14.40%	72855	8802	12.10%	591362	95942	16.20%
Jackson	75156	12004	16.00%	161537	15768	9.80%	33500	3609	10.80%	270193	31381	11.60%
Non-Metropolitan	**193312**	**36513**	**18.90%**	**428343**	**57796**	**13.50%**	**113645**	**15261**	**13.40%**	**735300**	**109570**	**14.90%**
Oscoda	42418	8756	20.60%	95149	13000	13.70%	29273	3999	13.70%	166840	25755	15.40%
Antrim	50926	7218	14.20%	112173	10085	9.00%	26463	2955	11.20%	189562	20258	10.70%
Wexford	38638	9220	23.90%	84723	14879	17.60%	21664	3096	14.30%	145025	27195	18.80%
Marquette	61330	11319	18.50%	136298	19832	14.60%	36245	5211	14.40%	233873	36362	15.50%
Michigan	**2424941**	**450426**	**18.60%**	**5597511**	**626186**	**11.20%**	**1054564**	**114086**	**10.80%**	**9077016**	**1190698**	**13.10%**

TABLE 8: PERSONS' POVERTY BY AGE BY LABOR MARKET AREAS, 1990

Source: Population Censuses, 1980 and 1990

Note: Columns 4, 7, and 10 show the poverty rates respectively for persons less than 18 years, 18 to 64 years, and more than 65 years of age. They are computed similarly using the formula (x / y)*100, where x is the number of persons of age x in poverty, and y is the total number of persons of age x for whom the poverty status was determined.

has stayed about the same and the proportion in metropolitan LMAs has declined slightly. The non-metropolitan LMAs have a significantly higher percentage of elderly residents. It follows, then, that the non-metropolitan LMAs have a smaller proportion of their population in the economically active age category of 15-64 years old.

In 1990 about one of every ten persons over sixty-four years old reported incomes at or below poverty. This represents a decrease in the poverty rate from 1980 (see table 7). The poverty rate of elderly residents in non-metropolitan LMAs is higher than in either mixed or metropolitan LMAs. Thus, regardless of age, personal poverty is highest among residents of non-metropolitan LMAs.

In contrast to this overall improved economic status of the elderly, the poverty rate for children has been increasing. In 1990 Michigan children under eighteen years old had a rate of 18.6 percent, compared to 10.8 percent for those persons sixty-five or older. In the Wexford LMA nearly one of every four children is in poverty. Across LMAs the personal poverty rates for children vary more than for the elderly (see table 8).

Family Poverty By Race. Native American and African-American families have higher rates of poverty than Caucasian families. Table 9 shows that in 1990, 5.4 percent of Caucasian families, 26.6 percent of African-American families, and 27.9 percent of Native American families were living in poverty. When we compare the poverty rates of families of different races, we find they are more vulnerable to poverty in different types of LMAs. Among Caucasian families, a higher poverty rate is found in mixed and non-metropolitan LMAs than in metropolitan LMAs. African-American families in mixed LMAs have a higher poverty rate than anywhere else. The highest poverty rates for African-American families are in Saginaw and Grand Rapids LMAs. The poverty rate for African American families in metropolitan LMAs is almost equal to that in non-metropolitan LMAs. In contrast to African-American and Caucasian families, Native American families in metropolitan LMAs have higher poverty rates. These differences also show that the economic vitality of an area may not benefit all groups the same.

When we examine the likelihood of families with children reporting poverty incomes, we find that families with children have slightly higher rates compared to all families. The families with children that are African-American or Native American have much higher poverty rates than Caucasian families. In 1990 39.8 percent of African-

TABLE 9: FAMILY POVERTY BY RACE BY LABOR MARKET AREAS, 1990

Labor market areas	Total number of White families	White families in poverty	% of White families in poverty	Total number of African-American families	African-American families in poverty	% of African-American families in poverty	Total Native American families	Native American families in poverty	% of Native American families in poverty
(1)	(2)	(3)	(4)	(5)	(6)	(7)	(8)	(9)	(10)
Metropolitan	1138304	52553	4.6%	261066	67366	25.8%	992	259	26.1%
Detroit	1032844	46597	4.5%	254044	65658	25.8%	658	188	28.6%
Lansing	105460	5956	5.6%	7022	1708	24.3%	334	71	21.3%
Mixed	633372	39183	6.2%	36662	11357	31.0%	3981	856	21.5%
Kalamazoo	141153	9070	6.4%	9624	2728	28.3%	490	133	27.1%
Grand Rapids	270732	13311	4.9%	15187	4432	29.2%	1239	149	12.0%
Saginaw	149785	12246	8.2%	9681	3606	37.2%	1303	232	17.8%
Jackson	71702	4556	6.4%	2170	591	27.2%	949	342	36.0%
Non-Metropolitan	280134	16986	6.1%	10019	2567	25.6%	4234	724	17.1%
Oscoda	48469	3920	8.1%	176	8	4.5%	1118	233	20.8%
Antrim	52518	2977	5.7%	53	13	24.5%	1496	243	16.2%
Wexford	155059	8164	5.3%	9787	2529	25.8%	1247	159	12.8%
Marquette	72557	5845	8.1%	179	25	14.0%	1491	322	21.6%
Michigan	2097734	113973	5.4%	306021	81374	26.6%	26554	7406	27.9%

Source: Population Censuses, 1980 and 1990

TABLE 10: FAMILIES WITH CHILDREN LESS THAN 18 IN POVERTY BY RACE BY LABOR MARKET AREAS, 1990									
Labor market areas	White families with children less than 18 years of age	White families with children less than 18 years of age in poverty	% of White families with children less than 18 years of age in poverty	African-American families with children less than 18 years of age	African-American families with children less than 18 years of age in poverty	% of African-American families with children less than 18 years of age in poverty	Native American families with children less than 18 years of age	Native American families with children less than 18 years of age in poverty	% of Native American families with children less than 18 years of age in poverty
(1)	(2)	(3)	(4)	(5)	(6)	(7)	(8)	(9)	(10)
Metropolitan	1015418	52553	5.2%	172551	67366	39.0%	868	259	29.8%
Detroit	921597	46597	5.1%	167489	65658	39.2%	584	188	32.2%
Lansing	93821	5956	6.3%	5062	1708	33.7%	284	71	25.0%
Mixed	564238	39183	6.9%	26008	11357	43.7%	3623	856	23.6%
Kalamazoo	126614	9070	7.2%	6609	2728	41.3%	455	133	29.2%
Grand Rapids	239208	13311	5.6%	11070	4432	40.0%	1137	149	13.1%
Saginaw	134166	12246	9.1%	6904	3606	52.2%	1168	232	19.9%
Jackson	64250	4556	7.1%	1425	591	41.5%	863	342	39.6%
Non-Metropolitan	248468	16986	6.8%	7390	2567	34.7%	3744	724	19.3%
Oscoda	43150	3920	9.1%	129	8	6.2%	989	233	23.6%
Antrim	46835	2977	6.4%	45	13	28.9%	1290	243	18.8%
Wexford	136621	8164	6.0%	7215	2529	35.1%	1111	159	14.3%
Marquette	65012	5845	9.0%	130	25	19.2%	1343	322	24.0%
Michigan	1872234	113973	6.1%	204482	81374	39.8%	23928	7406	31.0%

Source: Population Censuses, 1980 and 1990

American children were in families with incomes less than the poverty level. About one of every three families with Native American children was in poverty (see table 10).

LABOR FORCE STATUS

Employment. Full employment reflects greater opportunity in a labor market for workers to improve their economic livelihood. Most researchers include both employed and unemployed persons looking for work in the labor force. (The category of "not in the labor force" includes adults who are students, disabled, homemakers, and in the military.) In this study, we developed a measure of male and female employment rates—that is, the percentage of women or men ages fifteen to sixty-four who are employed.

In 1980 mixed LMAs had a higher rate of employment (90.4 percent) than the metropolitan (88.8 percent) and non-metropolitan (86.5 percent) LMAs. The Lansing and Grand Rapids LMAs presented the highest percentage of the civilian labor force employed (92.3 percent and 92 percent, respectively) while the Oscoda non-metropolitan LMA displayed the lowest percentage of its civilian labor force employed (84.1 percent).

In table 12 the employment status for Michigan adults in 1990 is shown. The percentage of the civilian labor force that was employed increased and the unemployment rate decreased between 1980 and 1990 in Michigan. However, the patterns of lower employment and higher unemployment rates in non-metropolitan LMAs in comparison to mixed and metropolitan LMAs continued.

For the state the male employment rate[15] was 70.4 percent and the female employment rate was 55.7 percent. As with the poverty rate, the levels of men and women employed were much lower in non-metropolitan LMAs than in metropolitan or mixed LMAs.

Female employment in Michigan increased from 48.8 percent in 1980 to 55.7 percent in 1990. Women in non-metropolitan LMAs were less likely to be in the labor force, although the gap is narrowing. As more women enter the non-metropolitan labor force they are confronted with higher unemployment than in other LMAs. In 1990 the non-metropolitan Wexford LMA had the highest unemployment rate among female workers. Women workers in the Lansing LMA reported the lowest unemployment rates.

TABLE 11: LABOR FORCE STATUS BY LABOR MARKET AREAS IN MICHIGAN, 1980

| Labor market areas | Total population 16 years + | Labor force number | % of adult population | Civilian labor force | | | Unemployed | | Not in labor force |
| | | | | Total | Employed number | % of labor force | number | % of labor force | |
(1)	(2)	(3)	(4)	(5)	(6)	(7)	(8)	(9)	(10)
Metropolitan	**4195260**	**2618513**	**62.4%**	**2614809**	**2321032**	**88.8%**	**293777**	**11.2%**	**1576747**
Detroit	3850290	2394737	62.2%	2391241	2114707	88.4%	276534	11.6%	1455553
Lansing	344970	223776	64.9%	223568	206325	92.3%	17243	7.7%	121194
Mixed	**1821049**	**1120895**	**61.6%**	**1119758**	**1012012**	**90.4%**	**107746**	**9.6%**	**700154**
Kalamazoo	421460	263137	62.4%	262837	239695	91.2%	23142	8.8%	158323
Grand Rapids	731976	464276	63.4%	463905	426815	92.0%	37090	8.0%	267700
Saginaw	457820	267507	58.4%	267146	232823	87.2%	34323	12.8%	190313
Jackson	209793	125975	60.0%	125870	112679	89.5%	13191	10.5%	83818
Non-Metropolitan	**549974**	**299328**	**54.4%**	**291807**	**252391**	**86.5%**	**39416**	**13.5%**	**250646**
Oscoda	117435	60473	51.5%	57557	48395	84.1%	9162	15.9%	56962
Antrim	126922	76112	60.0%	75749	66128	87.3%	9621	12.7%	50810
Wexford	112244	60098	53.5%	59950	52094	86.9%	7856	13.1%	52146
Marquette	193373	102645	53.1%	98551	85774	87.0%	12777	13.0%	90728
Michigan	**6873440**	**4224485**	**61.5%**	**4211997**	**3750732**	**89.0%**	**461265**	**11.0%**	**2648955**

Source: Population Censuses, 1980 and 1990

Note: Column 4 represents the percentage of adult population in labor force. It is computed as the total persons in labor force divided by the total population 16 years old and over. Column 7 represents the percentage of the civilian labor force which is employed, known as the employment rate. The employment rate is computed as the number of the civilian labor force employed divided by the total number in the civilian labor force. Column 9 shows the percentage of the civilian labor force unemployed. The unemployment rate equals the number of civilian labor force unemployed divided by the total number in the civilian labor force.

TABLE 12: LABOR FORCE STATUS BY LABOR MARKET AREAS IN MICHIGAN, 1990

Labor market areas	Total population 16 years +	Labor Force			Civilian labor force					
		number	% of adult population	% change labor force	Total	Employed number	% of labor force	Unemployed number	% of labor force	% change unemployed
(1)	(2)	(3)	(4)	(5)	(6)	(7)	(8)	(9)	(10)	(11)
Metropolitan	4261666	2763460	64.8%	3.9%	2758932	2523692	91.5%	235240	8.5%	-24.1%
Detroit	3898582	2513817	64.5%	3.7%	2509889	2290504	91.3%	219385	8.7%	-24.4%
Lansing	363084	249643	68.8%	6.0%	249043	233188	93.6%	15855	6.4%	-17.5%
Mixed	1941874	1254361	64.6%	4.9%	1252634	1159767	92.6%	92867	7.4%	-23.0%
Kalamazoo	442421	288027	65.1%	4.3%	287462	266344	92.7%	21118	7.3%	-16.6%
Grand Rapids	821754	553617	67.4%	6.2%	552951	519236	93.9%	33715	6.1%	-23.7%
Saginaw	461115	278726	60.4%	3.4%	278398	250379	89.9%	28019	10.1%	-21.7%
Jackson	216584	133991	61.9%	3.0%	133823	123808	92.5%	10015	7.5%	-28.6%
Non-Metropolitan	588219	336775	57.3%	5.2%	331398	299240	90.3%	32158	9.7%	-28.2%
Oscoda	131484	69675	53.0%	2.9%	67380	60429	89.7%	6951	10.3%	-35.2%
Antrim	146473	93396	63.8%	6.3%	93160	86171	92.5%	6989	7.5%	-40.9%
Wexford	116279	65962	56.7%	5.9%	65889	58300	88.5%	7589	11.5%	-12.1%
Marquette	193983	107742	55.5%	4.6%	104969	94340	89.9%	10629	10.1%	-21.9%
Michigan	7102020	4552382	64.1%	4.3%	4540537	4166196	91.8%	374341	8.2%	-24.7%

Source: Population Censuses, 1980 and 1990

Note: Column 4 represents the percentage of adult population in labor force. It is computed as the total number of persons in labor force divided by the total population 16 years old and over. Column 5 displays the percentage change of the labor force from 1980 to 1990. Column 8 represents the percentage of civilian labor force employed, known as the employment rate. The employment rate is computed as the number of the civilian labor force employed divided by the total number of the civilian labor force. Column 10 shows the percentage of the civilian labor force unemployed. The unemployment rate equals the number of civilian labor force unemployed divided by the total number of the civilian labor force. Column 11 contains the percentage change of the unemployment rate from 1980 to 1990.

A number of explanations have been offered for the lower levels of employment of women in non-metropolitan LMAs: non-metropolitan attitudes and values are more conservative and disapprove of women's employment; more households include married couples in non-metropolitan areas; and employment opportunities are more restricted in non-metropolitan LMAs.

Unemployment. The unemployment rate is defined as a percentage of the number of persons economically active or in the civilian labor force who are unemployed and looking for work. Non-metropolitan LMAs have a higher rate of unemployment, with 13.5 percent of the population unemployed, while metropolitan and mixed labor market areas have 11.2 percent and 9.6 percent unemployment rates, respectively. Also, we find some interesting differences among local LMAs of the non-metropolitan LMAs. Oscoda LMA workers report the highest level of unemployment of all state LMAs (including metropolitan LMAs), with a rate of 15.9 percent, compared with about 13 percent in the Oscoda, Antrim, and Marquette non-metropolitan LMAs.

Another indicator of economic distress in a labor market is the length of time it takes unemployed workers to find jobs. The periods of unemployment tend to be much longer in non-metropolitan LMAs than in metropolitan and mixed ones. In non-metropolitan LMAs, 48.7 percent of the unemployed have been unemployed fifteen weeks or more, compared with 38 percent of the unemployed in metropolitan and mixed LMAs. The Oscoda LMA has the highest percentage of unemployed workers who are unemployed for spells of fifteen weeks or more (53.3 percent). The average length of unemployment is shortest in the Lansing LMA.[16]

The unemployment rate reported in the 1990 Michigan census is lower than the rate found in 1980 throughout state LMAs. In 1980 state unemployment was at 11 percent, compared to 8.2 percent in 1990 (see tables 11 and 12). As one might expect, the LMAs with the greatest decline in unemployment also reported lower increases in poverty. For example, among non-metropolitan LMAs, Antrim area had a 40.9 percent decline in unemployment and a 11.7 percent increase in personal poverty over the decade. Wexford LMA had a 12.1 percent decline in unemployment and a 49 percent increase in personal poverty.

Female Employment Status. With the rise in female householders among families with children, female employment is a critical factor in the economic status of children. In addition, higher female

TABLE 13: FEMALE LABOR FORCE STATUS BY LABOR MARKET AREAS IN MICHIGAN, 1980

Labor market areas	Total population 16 years +	Labor force number	% of adult population	Civilian labor force			Unemployed	
				Total	Employed number	% of labor force	number	% of labor force
(1)	(2)	(3)	(4)	(5)	(6)	(7)	(8)	(9)
Metropolitan	2195522	1085676	49.4%	1085295	976423	90.0%	108872	10.0%
Detroit	2015842	988193	49.0%	987829	885172	89.6%	102657	10.4%
Lansing	179680	97483	54.3%	97466	91251	93.6%	6215	6.4%
Mixed	945708	465442	49.2%	465283	422000	90.7%	43283	9.3%
Kalamazoo	219936	112148	51.0%	112089	102752	91.7%	9337	8.3%
Grand Rapids	381081	194079	50.9%	194049	178380	91.9%	15669	8.1%
Saginaw	238300	107933	45.3%	107884	94919	88.0%	12965	12.0%
Jackson	106391	51282	48.2%	51261	45949	89.6%	5312	10.4%
Non-Metropolitan	278942	119448	42.8%	118817	104286	87.8%	14531	12.2%
Oscoda	60066	23647	39.4%	23411	19967	85.3%	3444	14.7%
Antrim	65864	31857	48.4%	31854	28019	88.0%	3835	12.0%
Wexford	57331	24529	42.8%	24526	21550	87.9%	2976	12.1%
Marquette	95681	39415	41.2%	39026	34750	89.0%	4276	11.0%
Michigan	3579992	1745295	48.8%	1744109	1569490	90.0%	174619	10.0%

Source: Population Censuses, 1980 and 1990

Note: Column 4 represents the percentage of adult population in labor force in 1980. It is computed as the total persons in labor force (3) divided by the total population 16 years old and over (2). Column 7 represents the percentage of the civilian labor force which is employed, known as the employment rate. The employment rate is computed as the number of the civilian labor force employed (6) divided by the total number in the civilian labor force (6). Column 9 shows the percentage of the civilian labor force unemployed. The unemployment rate equals the number of civilian labor force unemployed (8) divided by the total number in the civilian labor force (5).

TABLE 14: FEMALE LABOR FORCE STATUS BY LABOR MARKET AREAS IN MICHIGAN, 1990

Labor market areas	Total population 16 years +	Labor Force number	Labor Force % of population	% change labor force	Civilian Labor Force Total	Civilian Labor Force Employed number	Employed % of labor force	Unemployed number	Unemployed % of labor force	% change unemployed
(1)	(2)	(3)	(4)	(5)	(6)	(7)	(8)	(9)	(10)	(11)
Metropolitan	2246711	1259551	56.1%	13.4%	1258683	1157750	92.0%	100933	8.0%	-20.1%
Detroit	2056314	1141994	55.5%	13.3%	1141255	1047168	91.8%	94087	8.2%	-20.7%
Lansing	190397	117557	61.7%	13.8%	117428	110582	94.2%	6846	5.8%	-8.6%
Mixed	1006564	571130	56.7%	15.3%	570921	531469	93.1%	39452	6.9%	-25.7%
Kalamazoo	231554	133213	57.5%	12.8%	133162	124632	93.6%	8530	6.4%	-23.1%
Grand Rapids	423713	251441	59.3%	16.5%	251339	236049	93.9%	15290	6.1%	-24.7%
Saginaw	242191	125917	52.0%	14.8%	125885	114503	91.0%	11382	9.0%	-24.8%
Jackson	109106	60559	55.5%	15.2%	60535	56285	93.0%	4250	7.0%	-32.2%
Non-Metropolitan	298225	149667	50.2%	17.2%	148970	136036	91.3%	12934	8.7%	-29.0%
Oscoda	67748	30769	45.4%	15.4%	30443	27584	90.6%	2859	9.4%	-36.2%
Antrim	76094	42980	56.5%	16.8%	42961	39815	92.7%	3146	7.3%	-39.2%
Wexford	59312	29320	49.4%	15.5%	29313	26190	89.3%	3123	10.7%	-12.2%
Marquette	95071	46598	49.0%	19.0%	46253	42447	91.8%	3806	8.2%	-24.9%
Michigan	3713304	2068411	55.7%	14.3%	2066633	1907257	92.3%	159376	7.7%	-23.0%

Source: Population Censuses, 1980 and 1990

Note: Column 4 represents the percentage of adult population in labor force in 1990. It is computed as the total persons in labor force (3) divided by the total population 16 years old and over (2). Column 5 represents the percentage change of the labor force from 1980 to 1990. Column 8 represents the percentage of the civilian labor force which is employed, known as the employment rate. The employment rate is computed as the number of the civilian labor force employed (7) divided by the total number in the civilian labor force (7). Column 10 shows the percentage of the civilian labor force unemployed. The unemployment rate equals the number of civilian labor force unemployed (9) divided by the total number in the civilian labor force (6). Column 11 shows the percentage change of the civilian labor force unemployed from 1980 to 1990.

TABLE 15: EDUCATIONAL ATTAINMENT BY LMAs in 1990 (Persons 25 yrs and over)

Labor market areas	Elementary school	1-3 years high school	4 years high school	4 + years of college	Total	Elementary school	1-3 years high school	4 years high school	4 + years of college
(1)	(2)	(3)	(4)	(5)	(6)	(7)	(8)	(9)	(10)
Metropolitan	251598	553905	1052329	664266	2522098	10.0%	22.0%	41.7%	26.3%
Detroit	236487	523621	972470	599287	2331865	10.1%	22.5%	41.7%	25.7%
Lansing	15111	30284	79859	64979	190233	7.9%	15.9%	42.0%	34.2%
Mixed	130509	234405	553812	249342	1168068	11.2%	20.1%	47.4%	21.3%
Kalamazoo	26625	51594	120595	63986	262800	10.1%	19.6%	45.9%	24.3%
Grand Rapids	53336	96275	231995	111419	493025	10.8%	19.5%	47.1%	22.6%
Saginaw	37760	57732	135327	51136	281955	13.4%	20.5%	48.0%	18.1%
Jackson	12788	28804	65895	22801	130288	9.8%	22.1%	50.6%	17.5%
Non-Metropolitan	45743	73848	186705	66854	373150	12.3%	19.8%	50.0%	17.9%
Oscoda	12476	20237	44339	11356	88408	14.1%	22.9%	50.2%	12.8%
Antrim	8304	16608	45393	22096	92401	9.0%	18.0%	49.1%	23.9%
Wexford	9187	15291	37119	11106	72703	12.6%	21.0%	51.1%	15.3%
Marquette	15776	21712	59854	22296	119638	13.2%	18.1%	50.0%	18.6%
Michigan	452893	903866	1887449	1014047	4258255	10.6%	21.2%	44.3%	23.8%

Source: Population Censuses, 1980 and 1990

employment among married-couple families indicates increased economic potential. The female employment rate has increased steadily in all LMAs in Michigan. By 1990 well over half of women age sixteen and over were employed.

The female employment rate is lower in non-metropolitan LMAs. In 1990 50.2 percent of non-metropolitan women were employed, compared to 56.1 percent of women in metropolitan LMAs and 56.7 percent in mixed LMAs. But this gap is narrowing, with the female employment rates increasing to 17.2 percent in non-metropolitan LMAs, 15.3 percent in mixed LMAs, and 13.4 percent in metropolitan LMAs (see tables 13 and 14). Marquette non-metropolitan LMA had the highest increase in female employment over the last decade.

EDUCATION ATTAINMENT

Investments in education are expected to be associated with fuller employment and improved economic status of workers and their families. The educational attainment of Michigan adults differ slightly by LMA type. Non-metropolitan LMA residents over twenty-five years old are less likely to have attended or graduated from college. In 1980, 38 percent of Michigan residents twenty-five years or older reported less than four years of high school education. This dropped to 32 percent by 1990 (see table 15). In Michigan men's and women's educational attainment slightly differs, with men both slightly more likely to drop out of school before high school and more likely to have a college degree. Thus, there are not differences between labor market areas in educational attainment similar to the differences in employment and poverty. This suggests that without greater employment opportunities in labor market areas, workers with education are not able to earn incomes to bring their families out of poverty.

POVERTY, CHANGING EMPLOYMENT, AND FAMILY SIZE

Although the percentage of adults, particularly women, who are employed has increased and the general educational attainment has increased as well, average family size in Michigan has decreased and personal poverty rates have gone up over the past decade. The question to answer is what would the poverty rate be in 1990 if employment

TABLE 16: CHANGES IN FAMILY POVERTY ADJUSTED BY EMPLOYMENT RATE IN 1980 BY LABOR MARKET AREAS, 1980-1990

Labor market areas	Total families in 1980	Total families in poverty in 1980	% of families in poverty in 1980	Total families in 1990	Total families in poverty in 1990	% of families in poverty in 1990	Adjusted poverty rate in 1990
(1)	(2)	(3)	(4)	(5)	(6)	(7)	(8)
Metropolitan	**1451479**	**118644**	**8.2%**	**1452992**	**151954**	**10.5%**	**9.3%**
Detroit	1339407	110484	8.2%	1336148	141505	10.6%	9.4%
Lansing	112072	8160	7.3%	116844	10449	8.9%	8.3%
Mixed	**645635**	**51233**	**7.9%**	**685364**	**66098**	**9.6%**	**8.7%**
Kalamazoo	147077	11928	8.1%	153600	15060	9.8%	8.9%
Grand Rapids	261586	19020	7.3%	292824	23165	7.9%	7.3%
Saginaw	162733	14888	9.1%	163691	21104	12.9%	11.2%
Jackson	74239	5397	7.3%	75249	6769	9.0%	8.1%
Non-Metropolitan	**194118**	**18670**	**9.6%**	**207182**	**22952**	**11.1%**	**9.6%**
Oscoda	43943	4945	11.3%	49042	5878	12.0%	10.1%
Antrim	45884	3785	8.2%	53558	4282	8.0%	7.0%
Wexford	38951	4066	10.4%	40484	5519	13.6%	11.8%
Marquette	65340	5874	9.0%	64098	7273	11.3%	9.9%
Michigan	**2404910**	**198391**	**8.2%**	**2458481**	**251687**	**10.2%**	**9.1%**

Source: Population Censuses, 1980 and 1990

Note: Column 8 displays the family poverty rate in 1990 adjusted by employment rate in 1980. The adjusted family poverty rate in 1990 is computed as the family poverty rate in 1990 (column 7) multiplied by the employment rate in 1980 which is shown in column 7 of table 11.

TABLE 17: CHANGES IN FAMILY POVERTY ADJUSTED BY FAMILY SIZE BY LABOR MARKET AREAS, 1980-1990

Labor market areas	Total families in 1980	Total families in 1980 in poverty	% of families in poverty in 1980	Total families in 1990	Total families in 1990 in poverty	% of families in poverty in 1990	Adjusted poverty rate in 1990
(1)	(2)	(3)	(4)	(5)	(6)	(7)	(8)
Metropolitan	1451479	118644	8.2%	1452992	151954	10.5%	11.2%
Detroit	1339407	110484	8.2%	1336148	141505	10.6%	11.3%
Lansing	112072	8160	7.3%	116844	10449	8.9%	10.0%
Mixed	645635	51233	7.9%	685364	66098	9.6%	10.6%
Kalamazoo	147077	11928	8.1%	153600	15060	9.8%	10.2%
Grand Rapids	261586	19020	7.3%	292824	23165	7.9%	8.8%
Saginaw	162733	14888	9.1%	163691	21104	12.9%	14.8%
Jackson	74239	5397	7.3%	75249	6769	9.0%	9.7%
Non-Metropolitan	194118	18670	9.6%	207182	22952	11.1%	11.4%
Oscoda	43943	4945	11.3%	49042	5878	12.0%	11.8%
Antrim	45884	3785	8.2%	53558	4282	8.0%	8.4%
Wexford	38951	4066	10.4%	40484	5519	13.6%	13.9%
Marquette	65340	5874	9.0%	64098	7273	11.3%	11.9%
Michigan	2404910	198391	8.2%	2458481	251687	10.2%	11.0%

Source: Population Censuses, 1980 and 1990

Note: Column 8 displays the family poverty rate in 1990 adjusted by family size in 1980. The adjusted family poverty rate in 1990 is computed as the family poverty rate in 1990 (column 7) multiplied by the family size in 1980.

and family size had remained the same as they were in 1980? Table 16 provides family poverty rates adjusted by employment rates. The official family poverty rate in 1990 would have been 9.1 percent if employment patterns observed in 1980 had persisted through 1990. This is one percent below the observed family poverty rate. Moreover, the non-metropolitan adjusted poverty rate would remain higher than metropolitan and mixed poverty rates. Thus, we find that changing employment patterns have little effect on poverty rates in Michigan with practically no effect in non-metropolitan areas.

Table 17 shows family poverty rates adjusted by average family size in 1980. The official poverty rate would have increased more (11 percent) if family size in 1980 had remained the same in 1990. This implies that changes in family size have placed little downward pressure on poverty rates.

Changes in employment and family size of non-metropolitan families have had little effect on rates of poverty. Rather it may be that increasing poverty rates are more directly associated with changes in family structure and the economic returns from employment.

SUMMARY

Though the common image of economically distressed populations is of the poor metropolitan unemployed, our study documents how people living in non-metropolitan areas in Michigan are actually more vulnerable and more likely to experience economic distress and poverty than people in other areas. In Michigan the poverty rate—whether measured by personal, family, or per capita income—is higher in non-metropolitan LMAs than in mixed and metropolitan LMAs. For all age groups and family types, the chances of being in poverty are higher in non-metropolitan areas.

Our study shows that members of families headed by female householders, children, elderly residents, Native Americans and African Americans in non-metropolitan LMAs are more likely to live in poverty. The poverty rate of families with female householders increased throughout the state between 1980 and 1990. Non-metropolitan female householders are slightly more likely to live in poverty than those in metropolitan or mixed LMAs.

These findings paint an alarming picture for the children of Michigan, particularly those living in non-metropolitan areas.

Increasingly, Michigan children are highly likely to spend part of their childhood in poverty. In 1990 one of every six families with children had incomes less than the poverty threshold. One of every two Michigan female-headed households with children under eighteen years of age was in poverty.

Regardless of age, poverty rates are highest among residents of non-metropolitan LMAs. The number of elderly residents has increased over the past decade. Although the poverty rate of the elderly in Michigan in 1990 had decreased from 1980, the poverty rate of the elderly residents in non-metropolitan LMAs was higher than in either mixed or metropolitan LMAs. Yet, it is important to note that the improved status of the elderly represents an example of successful policies aimed at enhancing the economic status of a particular group in our population who was historically poor.

While more people in poverty are Caucasian, other racial groups are more vulnerable to economic distress. Native American and African-American families experience higher rates of poverty than Caucasian families. Among families with children under eighteen years of age, families with children that are African American or Native American have much higher poverty rates than Caucasian families.

Part of non-metropolitan poverty in Michigan can be explained by higher unemployment rates. Although the unemployment rate in Michigan decreased over the past decade, the unemployment rate is still higher in non-metropolitan LMAs than in metropolitan and mixed LMAs, and the length of unemployment is much longer in non-metropolitan LMAs than elsewhere. This is also reflected in lower employment rates in non-metropolitan LMAs.

Despite the fact that the percentage of the civilian labor force that is employed increased over the past decade in Michigan, personal poverty rates have increased by 38.7 percent. Likewise, educational attainment levels have shown steady increases. The female employment and adult educational attainment rates in Michigan have increased over the last decade in all LMAs in Michigan. Besides illustrating the difficulty in understanding poverty, we have also found that the way improved employment and education impact families differs and is uneven in its ramifications across different areas of the state.

POLICY IMPLICATIONS

Based on these aggregate findings of employment, unemployment, and education attainment, the economic status of Michigan families should show improvement. Higher education attainment signals greater investment in human capital in Michigan. More women are employed outside the home, and their income contributes to family incomes regardless of family structure. Why do we find such dramatic increases in family poverty? One possible explanation is that the economic returns for investment in education have dropped. The changing structure of employment opportunities in terms of occupations and industries suggests that more workers are in secondary occupations or peripheral industries. The increasing employment in service jobs will not be accompanied by higher incomes. Furthermore, gender wage discrimination and sex segregation in the work place continue to limit the earning potential for women and their ability to provide incomes to lift their families out of poverty.

One implication is that policies and programs may benefit some areas more than others. For example, more poor families in non-metropolitan areas are headed by married couples. Thus, non-metropolitan poor are less likely to benefit from changes in programs designed for female householders. Another example would be that extension of the length of time the unemployed can receive compensation would help more in non-metropolitan areas, where the length of unemployment tends to be longer. Clearly, non-metropolitan communities and counties have a more limited economic base for supporting mandated programs or developing sustenance programs based on local initiatives. These areas have lower per capita incomes and more limited employment opportunities, and therefore a much smaller tax base.

The social and economic well-being of non-metropolitan residents in Michigan is deteriorating. Poverty is a more common phenomenon in non-metropolitan LMAs than in mixed and metropolitan LMAs. Racial and ethnic minorities, the elderly, children, women and female-headed households in non-metropolitan LMAs are particularly disadvantaged. This study has policy implications for non-metropolitan development. Economic development does not benefit all. Policymakers need to consider uneven impact of economic development. Policies and programs designed for metropolitan areas should be different than those of non-metropolitan families since the social and economic conditions are different. Location is an important factor to consider in developing strategies to alleviate poverty in Michigan.[17]

NOTES

1. Gene Summers, ed., *Persistent Poverty in Rural America* (Boulder, Colorado: Westview Press, 1993); Daniel T. Lichter and David J. Eggebeen, "Child Poverty and the Changing Non-Metropolitan Family," *Rural Sociology Journal* 57, no. 2 (1992):151-72; Daniel T. Lichter, "Poverty and Employment: Impact on Rural Populations," *Briefing on Population Trends in Rural Areas* (Washington, D.C.: Northeast-Midwest Institute and the Population Resources Center, 1989); Cynthia M. Duncan, *Rural Poverty in America* (New York: Auburn House, 1992).

2. William Julius Wilson, *The Truly Disadvantaged: The Inner City, the Underclass, and Social Works* (Chicago: University of Chicago Press, 1987); Carol B. Stack, *All Our Kin: Strategy for Survival In a Black Community* (New York: Harper and Row, 1974).

3. Kenneth Deavers and Robert Hoppe, "Overview of the Rural Poor in the 1980s," in Cynthia M. Duncan, ed., *Rural Poverty In America* (New York: Auburn House, 1992).

4. Janet L. Bokemeier and Lorraine E. Garkovich, "Meeting Rural Family Needs," in Cornelia B. Flora and James A. Christenson, eds., *Rural Policies For the 1990s* (Boulder, Colorado: Westview Press, 1992).

5. Julie Strawn, "The States and the Poor: Child Poverty Rises as the Safety Net Shrinks," *Social Policy Report* 6, no. 3 (1992):1-22.

6. Aletha Huston, *Children in Poverty: Child Development and Public Policy* (Cambridge: Cambridge University Press, 1991).

7. Julie Strawn, "The States and the Poor."

8. Patrick Horan and Charles Tolbert III, *The Organization of Work in Non-metropolitan and Metropolitan Labor Markets* (Boulder Colorado: Westview Press, 1984); Ann R. Tickamyer and Janet L. Bokemeier, "Alternative Strategies for Labor Market Analyses: Micro-Macro Models of Labor Market Inequality," in Sigelman and Desoran, eds., *Inequality in Non-metropolitan Labor Markets* (Boulder, Colorado: Westview Press, 1992).

9. Lichter and Eggebeen, "Child Poverty."

10. See Charles M. Tolbert and Molly Sizer Killian, *Labor Market Areas For the United States* (Washington, D.C.: U.S. Department of Agriculture, Economic Research Service, Agriculture and Rural Economy Division, 1987).

11. In Michigan, 61 counties are classified as non-metropolitan (Social Science Research Bureau, 1990). These include counties in the Upper Peninsula, the northern Lower Peninsula, five counties that border Indiana and Ohio, and three counties on the eastern border of the state.

12. Official poverty is defined on the basis of whether family income from all sources (earnings, public assistance, etc.) is below poverty income thresholds

determined by an economic food plan for families of various sizes and unrelated individuals. The income cutoffs used by the Census Bureau to determine the poverty status of families and unrelated individuals included a set of 48 thresholds arranged in a two-dimensional matrix consisting of family size (from one person to nine or more persons) cross-classified by presence and number of family members under 18 years old (from no children present to eight or more children present). Unrelated individuals and two-person families were further differentiated by age of the householder (under 65 years and 65 years and over).

13. Lichter and Eggebeen, "Child Poverty."
14. See Janet L. Bokemeier and Jean Kayitsinga, *Metropolitan and Non-metropolitan Labor Markets in Michigan: Demographic Characteristics,* Research Report, Michigan State University, Agricultural Experiment Station, 1993, for details.
15. The male labor force participation rate is the total number of males employed divided by the total number of males in the civilian labor force. Similarly, the female labor force participation rate is the total number of females employed divided by the total number of females in the civilian labor force.
16. Bokemeier and Kayitsinga, *Metropolitan and Non-metropolitan Labor Markets in Michigan.*
17. This research was funded by Michigan Agricultural Experiment Extension, Michigan State University and the Economic Research Service of USDA. An earlier version of this article was prepared at the 1990 Census Briefing on Social and Economic Characteristics and Trends, Lansing, 24 March 1993.

REFERENCES

Bokemeier, Janet L., and Lorraine E. Garkovich. (1992). "Meeting Rural Family Needs." In Cornelia B. Flora and James A. Christenson (Eds.), *Rural Policies For the 1990s*. Boulder, Colorado: Westview Press.

Bokemeier, Janet L., and Jean Kayitsinga. (1993). *Metropolitan and Non-metropolitan Labor Markets in Michigan: Demographic Characteristics*. Research Report, Michigan State University, Agricultural Experiment Station.

Castle, Emery N. (1993). *Persistent Poverty in Rural America: Rural Sociological Society. Task Force on Persistent Rural Poverty*. Rural Studies Series. Boulder, Colorado: Westview Press.

Clogg, Clifford C., and Eliason R. Scott. (1988). "A Flexible Procedure for Adjusting Rates and Proportions, Including Statistical Methods for Group Comparisons." *American Sociological Review*. 53:267-83.

Coward, Raymond and Robert Jackson. (1982). "Environmental Stress: The Rural Family." In H. I. McCubbin, A. E. Cauble, and J. M. Patterson (Eds.), *Family Stress, Coping and Social Support*. Springfield, Illinois: Charles C Thomas.

Deavers, Kenneth, and Robert Hoppe. (1992). "Overview of the Rural Poor in the 1980s." In Cynthia M. Duncan (Ed.), *Rural Poverty in America*. New York: Auburn House.

Duncan, Cynthia M. (1992). *Rural Poverty in America*. New York: Auburn House.

Duncan, Greg J., and Willard L. Rodgers. (1991). "Has Children's Poverty Become More Persistent?" *American Sociological Review*. 56:538-50.

Eggebeen, David J., and Daniel T. Lichter. (1991). "Race, Family Structure, and Changing Poverty among American Children." *American Sociological Review*. 56:801-817.

Fitchen, Janet M. (1991). *Endangered Spaces, Enduring Places*. Boulder, Colorado: Westview Press.

Fitchen, Janet M. (1981). *Poverty in Rural America: A Case Study*. Boulder, Colorado: Westview Press.

Flora, C., and J. A. Christenson. (1992). *Rural Policies for the 1990s*. Boulder, Colorado: Westview Press.

Garrett, P., et al. (1993). "Rural Families and Children in Poverty." In Gene Summers (Ed.), *Persistent Poverty in Rural America*. Boulder, Colorado: Westview Press, 1993.

Hoppe, Robert A. (1991). "Defining and Measuring Poverty in Rural United States Using the Survey of Income and Program Participation." *Social Indicator Research*. 24:123-51.

Horan, Patrick, and Charles Tolbert II. (1984). *The Organization Work in Non-metropolitan and Metropolitan Labor Markets*. Boulder, Colorado: Westview Press.

Hughes, Robert J. (1987). "Empowering Rural Families and Communities." *Family Relation*. 36(4): 396-401.

Lichter, Daniel T., and David J. Eggebeen. (1992). "Child Poverty and the Changing Rural Family." *Rural Sociology Journal*. 57(2):151-72.

Lichter, Daniel T. (1989). "Poverty and Employment: Impact on Rural Populations." *Briefing on Population Trends in Rural Areas*. Northeast-Midwest Institute and the Population Resources Center, Washington, D.C.

Lichter, Daniel T. (1989). "Race, Employment Hardship, and Inequality in the American Non-metropolitan South." *American Sociological Review*. 54:436-46.

Lichter, Daniel T., and Janice A. Constanzo. (1987). Rural Underemployment and Labor-force Composition. *Rural Sociology*. 52:329-44.

Murdock, Steve H., and David R. Ellis. (1991). *Applied demography: An Introduction to Basic Concepts, Methods, and Data*. Boulder, Colorado: Westview.

Ruggles, Patricia. (1990). *Drawing the Line: Alternative Poverty Measures and Their Implications for Public Policy*. Washington, D.C.: Metropolitan Institute Press.

Stack, Carol B. (1974). *All our Kin: Strategy for Survival in a Black Community*. New York: Harper and Row.

Strawn, Julie. (1992). "The States and the Poor: Child Poverty Rises as the Safety Net Shrinks." *Social Policy Report*. 6(3):1-22.

Summers, Gene (Ed.). (1993). *Persistent Poverty in Rural America*. Boulder, Colorado: Westview Press.

Tickamyer, Ann R., and Janet L. Bokemeier. (1992). "Alternative Strategies for Labor Market Analyses: Micro-Macro Models of Labor Market Inequality." In Sigelman and Desoran (Eds.), *Inequality in Rural Labor Markets*. Boulder, Colorado: Westview Press.

Tickamyer, Ann R., and Janet L. Bokemeier. (1988). "Individual and Structural Explanations of Non-metropolitan Men and Women's Labor Force Experiences." In Falk, Lyson, and Schwarzweller (Eds.), *Research in Rural Sociology and Development*. vol. 3. Greenwich: JAI Press.

Tolbert, Charles M., and Molly Sizer Killian. (1987). *Labor Market Areas for the United States*. United States Department of Agriculture, Economic Research Service, Agriculture and Rural Economy Division.

Wilson, William Julius. (1987). *The Truly Disadvantaged: The Inner City, the Underclass, and Social Works.* Chicago: University of Chicago Press.

II.
Agriculture and Rural Policy

Rural Leadership, Knowledge, and Networks in Michigan: Can They Contribute to the Rural Policy Process?

Brendan Mullan

INTRODUCTION

The role of leadership, individual and institutional, has long been recognized in understanding the causes, content, and consequences of community change and cohesiveness. Recognition of the importance of individual and aggregate leadership in promoting and sustaining rural community political, social, and economic integration and vitality has grown significantly during the last two decades. When rural crisis engulfed the farm belt in the 1970s, agricultural leadership was widely recognized as the springboard for regaining vitality for rural and agricultural communities.[1]

In Michigan the importance of agricultural leaders and leadership in promoting and sustaining community development has become more widely recognized during the last two decades. Like other states with a substantial farm population, Michigan responded to the rural crisis of the 1970s by examining leadership channels and characteristics and identifying broad areas of concern among the local citizens relevant to the future vitality of the state's rural communities.[2] Unfriendly state and federal governments, the influence of large farm operators and adequate social and economic protection for families, farms, and communities were major concerns. The challenge remains one of involving agricultural and rural leaders in the policy process, but simply having these leaders identify problems is inadequate; their concerns must be recognized by policymakers and they must be actively included in the policymaking process and in the implementation of innovative solutions.

To facilitate a longitudinal comparison with earlier data and to identify current agricultural leaders and current leadership issues and concerns in rural Michigan, the Rural and Environmental Studies Group of the Department of Sociology at Michigan State University undertook a second leadership research project in the summer of 1991.

Preliminary analysis of the data collected from this research project identified some of the most critical issues facing rural Michigan today:

- Environmental and ecological issues ranging from groundwater contamination to agricultural chemicals causing damage to the local environment.
- Deteriorating socio-economic factors, the economic vitality of small towns, and the scale and scope of education provision.
- The concerns of individuals include the management and survival of rural farms, families, and communities, as well as a lack of cooperative communication with and among perceived leaders and leadership organizations.
- Lack of communication between individuals and organizations who are developing initiatives and activities to address the social, economic, ecological, and environmental issues identified as most pressing.

This article examines channels, networks, and patterns of communication among agricultural leaders in rural Michigan and assesses how that communication, and the associated spread of knowledge and good practice, contributes to deriving effective rural policy. This article further identifies mechanisms through which rural Michigan leaders can contribute their knowledge and experience to the policymaking process. The derivation and application of policy for rural Michigan can best be understood when it is placed within a data context. As was recently noted, "data drive policies, so it follows that a lack of information often results in non-responsive or biased public policies."[3] We utilize information from recently collected survey data to ask whether the rural policy making process can be enhanced by an understanding of the communication channels that exist among rural Michigan leaders. The paper concludes with a summary statement.

KEY POLICY QUESTIONS

A two-component framework is useful for conceptualizing the most salient issues facing rural Michigan:

- A component that consists of forces that internally affect farm operations. For example, issues related to off-farm work, gender role, household decision making patterns and farm family responses to rapidly changing societal, socio-political, and economic conditions. Basically, this component focuses on the individual and individual family responses to external forces as they affect the household unit and/or community.

- A component that consists of forces that, while not generated within the farm unit, exert tremendous pressure on farmers to change their knowledge, attitudes, and farming practices. These external forces cause farmers to modify their roles, behavior, and practices.

From these two dimensions we can list some of the key policy issues and questions facing rural farms, families, and communities:

- *Rural Outmigration.* Many potential rural leaders (farm and community) are leaving rural areas, and rural population growth lags behind the population growth of metropolitan areas.[4] It is well documented that "rural population trends are inversely correlated to community size—on average the smallest towns have been hardest hit, while mid-sized communities have come closer to holding their own."[5]

- *Demographic Processes.* Demographic changes (aging, migration, lower fertility and mortality, smaller families, and changing occupational characteristics and labor force participation patterns) among rural populations will have profound consequences in the coming

decades. The most rapidly growing segment of Michigan's population is that over the age of sixty-five, and this aging process is most
acute in rural areas. Furthermore, women make up the largest part
of this growing elderly population.

- *The Changing Nature of Farming.* There is a sharp dichotomy
  between the notions of "family farms" and "corporate farms."
  Conventional notions of family farms have become outmoded with
  increasing levels of off-farm labor force participation and changing
  gender roles. The role and function of corporate farming is closely
  bound with the impact of technical innovations on all aspects of
  the farming unit.

- *Technological Change.* The specific impacts of technical innovations
  involve three separate but interlinked phenomena: (1) the adoption
  of various technologies and biotechnologies, (2) the implementation and utilization of these technologies, and (3) the consequences
  of these technologies for rural families, farms, and communities.

The complexity of these issues and the speed at which changes are
occurring in rural Michigan are poorly understood by policymakers
but are very familiar to those occupying a leadership role in Michigan
agriculture. A central policy challenge is to include the knowledge and
the knowledge pathways extant among agricultural leaders into the
policymaking process. The first-hand knowledge, practices, and communication channels that exist among agricultural leaders (sometimes
referred to as local knowledge, or alternative knowledge) could provide solutions to some of the problems facing rural Michigan.

RURAL MICHIGAN LEADERSHIP, KNOWLEDGE, AND COMMUNICATION CHANNELS

The conventional view of the creation and dissemination of rural
agricultural scientific and community knowledge gives primacy to the
role of institutions. Knowledge creation and dissemination is a "top-
down" process. The role of institutional leadership has long been recognized as being of central importance in understanding the cause,
content, and consequences of innovation and change. For example,
the creation of the Land Grant colleges in 1862, the Agricultural
Experiment Station in 1887, and the Cooperative Extension Service in

1914, designed to promote formal and informal education of all forms, are long-established attempts to diffuse knowledge and technology within an institutional outreach paradigm.[6]

This is only one of two competing perspectives. The alternative contends that the Land Grant universities have:

> ... promoted and contributed to the development of an agricultural industry that inordinately benefits large agribusiness interests, gives large farmers unfair advantages over smaller farmers, contributes to the decline of rural communities, damages soil and water resources and exposes humans and other species to unsafe levels of dangerous chemical agents.[7]

The alternative view gives increased emphasis to the leadership role that local communities, individuals, and consumer advocates can play in creating and promoting "externalities" and "alternatives" to the accepted conventional wisdom of established knowledge producers. These groups nurture externalities and alternatives that can and do produce innovation at the local level. Policymakers ignore the innovative power and resourcefulness of such groups at their peril.

A polarization between proponents of the "conventional view" and the "alternative view" is evident, and the debate is just now beginning to move out of academic circles and into the lives and work of the people and organizations that constitute the core of rural America. Michigan is no exception to this broadening trend, and policymakers must include local communities, local political leaders, and community action groups as possible sources for innovative solutions to some of the key policy questions outlined at the beginning of this article.

Recent research has examined the nature and implications of local knowledge among academic faculty in Washington State and in Iowa.[8] The channels of knowledge generation and exchange in local communities, the local grassroots networks of communication, and the changing pattern and perception of local leadership all have a key role to play in understanding the competing and complementary roles of conventional versus alternative viewpoints. We know very little about how these channels and networks operate or how they contribute to the diffusion of new strategies for dealing with existing problems and stalemate situations. To paraphrase Kloppenburg, the policy challenge is to discover if and how these diverse nonacademic actors (agricultural leaders) create and contribute to knowledge solutions.[9] To address this challenge, this article conceptually specifies, operational-izes, and empirically examines several policy-relevant research questions originating from this alternative perspective.

There is a growing consensus that it is inappropriate to view local agricultural leadership initiatives as merely reacting to agri-industrial technology and economics. An industrial version (also described as "journalistic-commercial") of agriculture and rural life exists in which the "private knowledge, judgment, and effort" of the farmer and the consumer can be "satisfactorily replaced by generalized, expensive, technological solutions."[10] Furthermore, these solutions are not based upon an understanding of local requirements or conditions, but come with the imprimatur of industrial corporations, governments, and universities. This industrial agriculture dismisses the power, sophistica-tion, and expertise of the agricultural and rural mind. The concept of "ordinary excellence"[11] is of paramount importance in understanding how individuals master and implement extremely complicated infra-structure management, animal management, and other techniques of modern farming and rural survival in general.

A series of generalized questions focusing on the nature and con-tent of local rural knowledge have been proposed.[12] This series of questions covers the most salient issues related to the causes, content, and consequences of local knowledge and serves as a benchmark agenda. From a policy perspective, this article uses sample data to focus on two of these issues:

1. How is local knowledge influenced by external and internal infor-mation sources?
2. How might farmers' knowledge be used to complement scientists' knowledge and vice-versa, and how can farmer-scientist interac-tions be facilitated and managed in such a way that this comple-mentarity is best realized?

During the spring and summer of 1991, with the close cooperation of the Cooperative Extension Service, an exploratory study was under-taken with the aim of identifying some of the issues and problems fac-ing the "future vitality of rural communities and the farming industry in Michigan."[13] From this survey over 1,008 people were identified through a process of referral as influential and respected agricultural leaders in their local communities. From this list of names, 256 indi-viduals were randomly selected for a follow-up telephone interview during the winter of 1992-93.[14]

Essentially, the compilation of the final sample used referral sampling techniques. This sampling technique is appropriate when difficult-to-enumerate populations are the focus of study and the creation of an adequate sampling frame is untenable. The sample was stratified to ensure that it was evenly distributed geographically in order to have equal representation of all segments of Michigan's population. Furthermore, the gender distribution is reflective of the population, with almost equal gender proportions sampled.[15]

The interview schedule itself consisted of five modules. The first focused on leadership characteristics, attitudes, and qualities. The second sought to identify important community issues and individuals' responses to those issues. The third elicited information on attitudes toward, and issues confronting, women leaders. The fourth ascertained information on the extent and utilization of leadership communication channels. Finally, we concluded with a conventional collection of respondents' basic demographic characteristics. Comprehensive reliability and validity checks were run on all items and, with very few exceptions, we are confident that despite the reputational/referral nature of the sample creation, the data do reflect knowledge, attitudes, and practices related to leadership throughout Michigan.

AGRICULTURAL LEADERS IN MICHIGAN

A range of basic demographic and socio-economic questions provides the basis for developing an overall profile of the 256 individuals who make up the sample. In brief, this sample is of rural leaders who were well educated. Over 60 percent had some college-level education, and 23.6 percent of the women and 31.6 percent of the men have college degrees. These leaders are economically well-off—69 percent have an annual household income above $40,000. Forty-eight percent of the respondents were female. Although male leaders were slightly more likely to have college degrees and incomes in excess of $40,000, the difference between genders is not statistically significant.[16] However, there were significant gender differences in terms of age, occupation, and background characteristics. Men were more likely than women to indicate their occupations as farmer and to have had fathers who were farmers. It is likely that many women who work on farms did not classify themselves as farmers. The mean age of male and female leaders was quite similar, but there were more men under age 35 and over age 65 than women.

INTERNAL AND EXTERNAL INFORMATION SOURCES

The data for this article do not permit an explicit examination of whether or not rural individuals' acquisition and application of skills and knowledge is differentially influenced by internal (local knowledge exchanges and self-taught experiential knowledge) or external (institutional, university, or government-sponsored research) knowledge. Detailed, individual case study research will eventually facilitate such a detailed examination. However, the data do permit an examination of how often individuals work with local or extra-local groups, thereby enabling a comparison of the importance of contact with internal and external knowledge sources.

We measure these internal and external contacts using two different operationalizations, frequency of contact and perceived importance of support. For internal knowledge, the frequency of contact among rural leaders (weekly, monthly, or never) provides one operationalization, and the perceived importance of having the support of fellow leaders (very important, somewhat important, or unimportant) provides a second operationalization.

For external knowledge a distinction is drawn between the external knowledge originating in scientific institutions, universities, and county agricultural extension offices, which we call external institutional knowledge, and the external knowledge originating from industrial and commercial sources (e.g. food processing conglomerates and commodity groups), which we call external agribusiness knowledge. Again, we have two operationalizations using frequency of contact between the agricultural leaders and these external sources and the perceived support the leaders feel they receive from these external sources. The percentage of respondents reporting frequency of contact with, and perceived support derived from, internal and external knowledge sources, controlling for geographic region, is reported in table 1.

Table 1 clearly shows that agricultural leaders have much more contact with internal knowledge producing sources, such as fellow leaders, agricultural workers, and local community residents, irrespective of region. Weekly contact with internal sources far outstrips weekly

Table 1. Frequency of Involvement with, and Perceived Importance of Support Derived from, Internal and External (Local and Extra-Local) Knowledge Sources, Michigan 1992-1993.

	North	N.West	East	West	L Central	S.East	S.West	TOTAL
Internal Sources								
Weekly	18.6	25.0	32.3	12.5	31.0	35.6	31.6	26.2
Monthly	67.4	58.3	51.6	72.5	42.9	46.7	42.1	55.5
Infreq/Never	14.0	16.7	16.1	15.0	26.2	17.8	26.3	18.4
External Institutional Sources								
Weekly	11.6	19.4	19.4	12.5	9.5	11.1	10.5	13.3
Monthly	51.2	52.8	35.5	57.5	47.6	51.1	57.9	50.4
Infreq/Never	37.2	27.8	45.2	30.0	42.9	37.8	31.6	36.3
External Agri-Business Sources								
Weekly	7.0	8.3	9.7	5.0	7.1	11.1	15.8	8.6
Monthly	32.6	61.1	41.9	25.0	28.6	35.6	15.8	35.2
Infreq/Never	60.4	30.6	48.4	70.0	64.3	56.3	68.4	56.3
Internal Support Sources								
Unimportant	--	--	--	--	--	--	5.3	0.4
Somewhat Important	20.9	13.9	6.5	12.5	16.7	17.8	--	14.1
Very Important	79.1	86.1	93.5	87.5	83.3	82.2	94.7	85.5
External Institutional Support Sources								
Unimportant	2.3	--	--	5.0	--	2.2	5.3	2.0
Somewhat Important	67.4	58.3	58.1	60.0	50.0	51.1	47.4	56.6
Very Important	30.2	41.7	41.9	35.0	50.0	46.7	47.4	41.4
External Agri-Business Support Sources								
Unimportant	4.7	8.3	6.5	2.5	7.1	4.4	10.5	5.9
Somewhat Important	58.1	30.6	61.3	55.0	47.6	51.1	52.6	50.8
Very Important	37.2	61.1	32.3	42.5	45.2	44.4	36.8	43.4
N	43	36	31	40	42	45	19	256

contact with external institutional sources and the lowest weekly contact percentages are with external agribusiness. Only in southwest Michigan, where agribusiness concerns tend to be headquartered, does the contact percentage with agribusiness increase, and even here it approaches only 16 percent. Conversely, the percentage of respondents reporting no contact or infrequent contact with both the external knowledge sources far exceeds the corresponding figures for internal knowledge contacts.

Table 1 provides further evidence of individuals' greater familiarity with local sources of knowledge and expertise than with external knowledge bases. With the single exception of the southwest corner of the state, no respondent rates the support received from other local leaders, agricultural workers, and local community residents as unimportant, and the percentages rating the support of both institutional and agribusiness external knowledge producers as very important are significantly lower.

Even with the caveats of the indirect operationalization procedures kept firmly in mind, this table provides concrete evidence that local agricultural leaders have much more contact with, and derive stronger support from, fellow leaders, farmers, and other local knowledge producing sources than with external institution sources, i.e. university, government, or agribusiness. In itself this is an unremarkable finding: policymakers would expect no less. But if it is plausible to suggest that where contact and support are greatest (knowledge creation, exchange, experimentation, refinement, and implementation will occur to the greatest effect) then direct empirical evidence of very strong local contact and support mechanisms lends support to the idea that successful policy derivation and implementation depend on the links between innovation and local knowledge.

COMMUNICATION CHANNELS AMONG AGRICULTURAL LEADERS

The second research question identified as pertinent for this discussion asks how farmer-scientist interactions can be facilitated and managed in such a way that local agricultural leaders' knowledge may be used to complement scientists' knowledge, and vice versa. Our approach to this question is to describe what means of communication and information exchange local individuals find most effective.

Understanding what the most effective channels of communication are among individuals and between individuals and various external institutions will facilitate the creation and implementation of highly effective information exchange mechanisms and networks.

The Michigan Rural Survey contained a battery of questions aimed at eliciting information on the extent and utilization of communication channels among the respondents and between the respondents and a range of outside organizations. Respondents were asked to rate the effectiveness of eight different communication channels: local newspapers, local workshops/seminars sponsored by local farmers and community groups, statewide newspapers, statewide workshops/seminars sponsored by the Department of Agriculture, workshops/seminars sponsored by the county extension office, short workshops/seminars sponsored by Michigan State University, and week-long expos and programs sponsored by MSU.

With the effectiveness scale ranging from very effective, to somewhat effective, to ineffective, these individual items were variously combined to create composite measures assessing the effectiveness of internal communication channels (local newspapers and local workshops/seminars), external institutional communication channels (county extension office or MSU-sponsored seminars/workshops/expos), and external government communication channels (Department of Agriculture workshops/seminars and state newspapers). The percentage of respondents reporting their effectiveness ratings for each of these composite measures are reported in table 2, with controls added for region. The highest ineffective percentages are reported for the external government communication channels, which primarily consist of Department of Agriculture-sponsored seminars and workshops, although overall this information exchange mechanism receives a high rating as being somewhat effective. The most effective means of communication is the external institutional-sponsored workshops, seminars, and expos. It is likely that these events facilitate information exchange along multiple dimensions. They undoubtedly serve to describe and disseminate the work of the county extension offices and the Land Grant university, but also such events serve as a central forum where motivated individuals meet each other and exchange knowledge and information. An example of such an event is the Agriculture and Natural Resources week-long series of displays, expositions, seminars, social events, and meetings sponsored by Michigan State University each spring.

Table 2.   Reported Effectiveness of Communication at the Local and Extra-Local Level, by Region, Michigan 1992-1993.

	North	N.West	East	West	L. Central	S. East	S. West	TOTAL
Internal Communication Channels								
Ineffective	9.3	11.1	3.2	5.0	--	4.4	5.3	5.5
Somewhat Effective	67.4	66.7	80.6	57.5	61.9	68.9	78.9	67.6
Very Effective	23.3	22.2	16.1	37.5	38.1	26.7	15.8	27.0
External Institutional Communication Channels								
Ineffective	4.7	2.8	--	--	2.4	--	--	1.6
Somewhat Effective	60.5	55.6	51.6	42.5	40.5	53.3	36.8	49.6
Very Effective	34.9	41.7	48.4	57.5	57.1	46.7	63.2	48.8
External Journalistic Communication Channels								
Ineffective	11.6	8.3	9.7	12.5	4.8	11.1	5.3	9.4
Somewhat Effective	76.7	83.3	77.4	75.0	83.3	80.0	84.2	79.7
Very Effective	11.6	8.3	12.9	12.5	11.9	8.9	10.5	10.9
N	43	36	31	40	42	45	19	256

The primary finding of this table is the high rating of effectiveness of all three composite channels of communication—only in very few cases are these rated as ineffective by more than 10 percent of respondents. Behind this observation lies an intriguing conundrum. If these various channels of communication are so effective, why is it that in what few case studies exist on the creation and implementation of local knowledge-based farming systems (e.g., rotational grazing in Wisconsin), it is persuasively argued that the creation of this knowledge base is "taking place almost completely outside the formal scientific institutions of agricultural research"?[17] Perceived effectiveness is no substitute for content effectiveness. Possibly, existing channels of information exchange do not yet include discussions, descriptions, and critiques of local knowledge. Local knowledge systems and expertise are not included as part of the currently accepted methods of communications.

SUMMARY

It has recently been noted that the policy uses of rural data are likely to increase at the national and state levels because of greater statistical literacy among program planners, government and corporate executives, legislators, and the public at large and because of the greater availability of sophisticated rural databases of all kinds.[18] Furthermore, this opinion is applicable to both secondary analysis of population data and to the analysis of original survey data. Topic-specific and target-specific survey data are now either readily available or easily commissioned, and with the application of basic statistical and methodological techniques, trends and patterns are readily discernible and can be used as input to informed policy decision making. Within Michigan there have been several publications focusing on rural areas and the special problems and issues related to those areas. This article has drawn upon a specially commissioned survey data set to examine if and/or how the process of information creation, knowledge dissemination, and networks among individuals at the grassroots level in rural Michigan can contribute to the policy debate.

During the twentieth century, "public agricultural research, extension, and educational investments have been focused mainly on technology, while farm and rural people have been benignly neglected."[19] One consequence of this neglect is the increasing relevance of social science for understanding and suggesting solutions to the challenges and problems confronting rural society. An initial response to this challenge was the 1991 Social Science Agricultural (and Rural) Agenda Project (SSAAP), which attempts to identify where social science approaches can contribute to understanding rural issues. The SSAAP report specifically states that the "U.S. agenda of rural problems is dominated by unintended externalities, the consequences of obsolescent and failed institutions, and the need for higher quality human capital."[20] The report further calls for the inclusion of different kinds of knowledge as a research and policy-generating dimension.

The data analyzed in this article show the importance of including local rural leaders' knowledge in the policymaking process. The article focuses on the extent of communication between leaders and in leaders' external communication with external institutional and government entities. In short, the changing content, character, and communication channels of Michigan's rural leadership, and the increased sophistication resulting from these changes, mandates that the policy initiatives planned by state legislators and policymakers at all levels now incorporate input and response from the local grassroots leaders. The demand for social and economic services and Michigan's ability to provide the requisite range of services will be a dynamic reciprocal process between communities and central bureaucracies.

The data to monitor the causes and predicted paths of these reciprocal relationships are becoming available—the policy response is the challenge.[21]

NOTES

1. For example, see Thomas A. Lyson, Harry K. Schwarzweller, and J. Allan Beegle, *Problems and Issues Confronting Rural Michigan: Agri-Leaders Look Toward the '80s*, Michigan State University Agricultural Experiment Station Research Report no. 357, 1978; Thomas Koebernick and J. Allan Beegle, *Selected Attitudes and Opinions of Michigan's Rural Population*, Michigan State University Agricultural Experiment Station Research Report no. 169, 1972; William J. Kimball, Manfred Thullen, Alan Kirk, and Christopher Doozan, *Community Needs and Priorities as Revealed by the Michigan Public Opinion Survey*, Extension Bulletin E-1082, Cooperative Extension Service, Michigan State University, 1977.
2. Lyson, Schwarzweller, and Beegle, *Problems and Issues Confronting Rural Michigan*.

3. James A. Christenson, Richard Maurer, and Nancy L. Strang, eds., *Rural, Data, People, & Policy*, Rural Studies Series (Boulder, Colorado: Westview Press, 1994), 2.

4. Kenneth L. Deavers, "Rural Development in the 1990's: Data and Research Needs," Paper prepared for the Rural Social Science Symposium, AAEA, Baton Rouge, Louisiana, 28-29 July 1989, 11; Calvin L. Beale and Glenn V. Fuguitt, "Decade of Pessimistic Nonmetro Population Trends Ends on Optimistic Note," *Rural Development Perspectives* 6, no. 3 (1990):14-18.

5. William Gallston, "Rural America in the 1990's: Trends and Choices," in *Population Change and the Future of Rural America*, edited by Linda Swanson and David L. Brown, Agriculture and Rural Economy Division, Economic Research Service, U.S. Department of Agriculture, Staff Report no. AGES 9324, 1993.

6. Curtis E. Beus and Riley Dunlap, "The Alternative-Conventional Agriculture Debate: Where Do Agricultural Faculty Stand?" *Rural Sociology* 57, no. 3 (1992); Jack Kloppenburg Jr. "Social Theory and the De/Reconstruction of Agricultural Science: Local Knowledge for an Alternative Agriculture," *Rural Sociology* 56, no. 4 (1991).

7. Beus and Dunlap, "The Alternative-Conventional Agriculture Debate."

8. Beus and Dunlap, "The Alternative-Conventional Agriculture Debate"; G. Bultena and P. Lasley, "The Dark Side of Agricultural Biotechnology," in *Agricultural Bioethics: Implications of Agricultural Biotechnology*, edited by S. Gendel, A. D. Kline, D. M. Warren, and F. Yates (Ames: Iowa State University Press, 1990).

9. Kloppenburg Jr., "Social Theory and the De/Reconstruction of Agricultural Science."

10. Wendell Berry, "Whose Head is the Farmer Using?: Whose Head is Using the Farmer?" in *Meeting the Expectations of the Land: Essays in Sustainable Agriculture and Stewardship* (San Francisco: North Point Press, 1984), 23.

11. Ibid., 27

12. Kloppenburg, Jr., "Social Theory and the De/Reconstruction of Agricultural Science"; N. Hassanein, "As You Know . . .: Farmer's Knowledge and Sustainable," *As You Sow . . . Social Issues in Agriculture* no. 29 (April 1993).

13. Harry K. Schwarzweller and Elizabeth M. Roach, *Issues and Problems Confronting Rural Michigan in the '90s*, Michigan State University Agricultural Experiment Station Research Report 530, 1993.

14. As reported in Schwarzweller and Roach, (*Issues and Problems Confronting Rural Michigan in the '90s*, 2), the sampling frame consisted of a list of all county extension directors, agricultural agents, home economists, and district agents in Michigan. This list was supplemented with representatives of four major farmers groups, Farm Bureau county presidents, National Farmers' Organization leaders, state Grange leaders, and Women for the Survival of Agriculture in Michigan. In total, completed questionnaires were received from 133 Extension Service respondents and from 119 representatives of the four major farm organizations. Information from the survey enabled thematic identification of the main concerns being expressed by extension agents and by farm organization representatives.

15. To ensure geographic representation, Michigan was divided into seven zones on the basis of zip codes, with each zone containing an approximately equal number of respondents. Taking into account refusals, ineligible respondents, and non-working telephone numbers, the study ended with a completion rate of 74 percent and a very low refusal rate of 3 percent. The telephone interview length ranged from 16 to 108 minutes with an average interview length of 26.32 minutes. Despite our attempts to equalize selection probabilities within region, affiliation, and gender, we acknowledge that sampling error may be problematic given the non-random origins of the initial population; consequently, inferential analyses are kept to a minimum.
16. All tests of significance are carried out with an alpha set to .05.
17. Kloppenburg Jr., "Social Theory and the De/Reconstruction of Agricultural Science"; Hassanein, "As You Know . . ."
18. Christenson, Maurer, and Strang, *Rural, Data, People, & Policy*.
19. Glenn L. Johnson, James T. Bonnen, Darrell Fienup, C. Leroy Quance, and Neill Schaller, *Social Science Agricultural Agendas and Strategies* (East Lansing: Michigan State University Press, 1991), xiii.
20. Ibid., I-9.
21. This research is supported by funds from the Michigan Agricultural Experiment Station. The author wishes to acknowledge the valuable research assistance of Elaine Allensworth, MSU Department of Sociology.

Mapping the Middle Road for Michigan Pest Management Policy

Craig K. Harris and Mark E. Whalon

INTRODUCTION

For most of this century, public policy concerning the management of agricultural pests has been a subject of controversy. From worries in the 1920s and 1930s about the toxicity of inorganic compounds like lead arsenate for human consumers, the focus has shifted to concerns about impacts on non-target species in the 1960s and 1970s following *Silent Spring*, and more recently to threats to agricultural sustainability from pest resistance. These concerns have been particularly important for Michigan because of the significance of fruit and vegetable production to Michigan's economy.

In the past, diversity has been a major strength of Michigan's agriculture. Diversity has enabled Michigan's agriculture to endure fluctuations in climate and market. However, that diversity is now becoming the Achilles' heel of Michigan agriculture because the management of pests requires the development of intensive techniques for specific crops in particular geoclimatic settings. Developing these techniques may require levels of investment beyond the willingness and/or ability of agro-industry, public institutions, or individual growers.

Pest management policy in Michigan ought to provide growers with information and practices that enable them to adapt to the dynamic confluence of changing markets, shifting consumer demands, evolving and exotic pests, and changing regulations. This requires an anticipation of what will be the nature of the market, the physical and biological environment, government policy at some point in the future, and the allocation of research and development capacity to meet the requirements of those conditions. Current policy, however, is often focused on the past and the present, not the future. Rather than anticipate the needs of the future, current policy is designed to avoid the problems of the past and comply with the requirements of the present. This may be a short-sighted position if tomorrow is quite different from today or yesterday.

If pest management policy in Michigan is to be effective, it must focus on the problems and demands of the future—international markets, ecological marketing and other niche markets, loss of key chemicals, and pest resistance. It must facilitate transitions by growers from outmoded pest management regimes to sustainable approaches. Pest management techniques to meet these needs can best be developed if research is guided by all the significant stakeholders in the agricultural system.

In this article, we focus on pest management issues in agriculture; while use of insecticides, fungicides, and herbicides is significant in the residential, commercial, industrial, and government sectors, in all cases the predominant user is agriculture. Within agriculture, we focus on the production of fruit and vegetables in Michigan, since the issues of pest management intersect most strongly in those enterprises. At the same time, we do not focus on any particular kinds of pests; we will use the term to refer to the full range of insects, fungi, diseases, nematodes, and weeds that diminish the quantity or quality of agricultural production or interfere with the maintenance of that production after it is harvested. We first describe the agricultural system and the current policies that govern pest management. We then discuss several forces that are pushing pest management policies in divergent directions. We outline three alternative outcomes that might result from the effects of these forces. Finally, we suggest a set of changes in pest management policy that will enable Michigan agriculture to adapt to the constraints and opportunities of the future.

FRUITS AND VEGETABLES IN MICHIGAN AGRICULTURE

When Michigan agriculture is considered, it is the fruit and vegetable crops that make it distinctive. The produce from Michigan's farms is the third most diverse in the nation, after California and Florida, largely because of the fruits and vegetables produced here. This diversity in farm production carries over into food processing, since several major firms are located in Michigan primarily to process fruit and vegetables. This diversity also makes Michigan agriculture very distinct from that of our neighboring states, which have a much higher prevalence of corn and soybean production. These fruit and vegetable crops attract farm laborers for employment and tourists for recreation.

History of fruit and vegetable crops in Michigan. Although some have suggested that Johnny Appleseed was the founder of the Michigan fruit industry, it was actually peaches that first came to prominence in the state. From the late 1800s on, peaches were a major crop along the western edge of the Lower Peninsula, both for fresh markets and for processing. From the 1920s through the 1950s, pears were prominent in the same region, often grown on the same farms. It was not until the 1960s, however, that apples became significant, but they quickly surpassed peaches and pears in importance. At the same time, tart and sweet cherries became important, and by 1980, tart cherries had become the most valuable crop produced in the state.

While the tree fruit industry was developing in the area west of the Grand Rapids ridge, the small fruit industry was developing in the southwest corner of the state. Taking advantage of the protection from severe cold afforded by the proximity to Lake Michigan, blueberries were established in areas with boggy soils. Grape vineyards were planted in the rolling topography of the southwest region. Strawberries were also successful in this area and were usually produced in conjunction with other small fruits. The well-drained soils were also well suited to raspberries, blackberries, and other cane fruits.

Markets. The fruit and vegetables produced in Michigan are exchanged in a variety of markets. The most important distinction is between fresh and processed. In general, produce for the fresh market must meet higher appearance standards than that for processing. Recent years have witnessed the extension of the calendar for the fresh market with controlled atmosphere storage and major challenges in the fresh market from counter-seasonal production in the southern hemisphere. The fresh market includes produce sold to packers and shippers for wholesaling to retailers and distributors, produce sold directly by the grower to retailers and preparers, and produce sold directly to consumers at farmers' markets, roadside markets, or u-pick operations. Processing of fruit and vegetables continues to be important in the canned and frozen foods industries, particularly in the food service and private market segments.

The second way in which produce markets are divided is into domestic and international destinations. Currently, with the exception of Canada, international markets are not very significant. Although apples are one of Michigan's major fruit crops, exports of Michigan apples to the United Kingdom account for less than 1 percent of European apple consumption. Nevertheless, other states where fruit and vegetable production is prominent have negotiated sizeable export deals, and the passage of the North American Free Trade Agreement (NAFTA) could increase exports of Michigan vegetables to Canada and Mexico (fruit was exempted from the treaty).

Markets for Michigan's fruit and vegetable produce are also divided into general markets and niche markets. General markets are characterized by low differentiation; sweet cherries are sweet cherries, and peaches are peaches. Niche markets can be created along any number of dimensions. Although not numerically significant, one of the most prominent is the organic market; less than 2 percent of the fruit and vegetables produced in Michigan are certified organically grown.[1] An emerging dimension of importance is variety; one of the attractions of farmers' markets is the ability to obtain older varieties of apples, traditional varieties of cucumbers, etc.

THE AGRICULTURAL SYSTEM AND CURRENT PEST MANAGEMENT POLICY

The agricultural system. While pest management policy is situated within the agricultural sector, agriculture is much more than farms and the people who work on them. In our view, growing fruit is one of several activities that make up the agriculture and food system (see figure 1). The ten components of this system are interrelated by the products and money that they exchange, by the information that flows between them, and by the battles they fight over pest management policy. We will discuss each of the components briefly and then

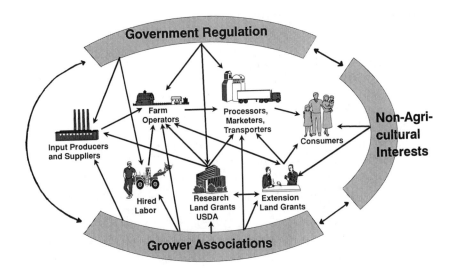

Figure 1. The Agricultural System.

describe the current pest management policies that have resulted from the operation of this system.

Fruit farm operators and their farms are at the center of the system and are linked with all of the other elements in the system. The grower may be only one person, or the operation of the fruit farm may involve several members of the farm family. The farm may specialize in one or two fruit crops, or fruit may be one of several commodities raised on a diversified farm. The farm may be an individual or family proprietorship, or it may be a corporation. For the principal operator, the fruit farm may be a full-time or part-time occupation.

Producing the fruit crop each year requires several types of inputs. Some of these are chemicals or machinery that come from agribusinesses via local retailers or cooperatives. Other inputs are money for acquiring land or new rootstock or to buy the materials needed for the annual production cycle; money may come from local banks or government loan programs.

Unless the farm family can provide all the labor needed to produce the crop, the grower must hire farm labor. These may be local temporary workers hired on a short-term basis for specific operations like picking. They may be migrant laborers, either from Michigan or else-where, hired directly or through a crew organizer. As the activities of fruit production expand to extend more evenly throughout the year, it is more likely that hired labor will be regular, full-time, skilled employees receiving compensation comparable to that of other skilled workers so that growers can retain the services of high quality labor.[2]

Unless the grower has on-farm storage, the crop leaves the farm after it is harvested and goes to processors and/or marketers and trans-porters. Marketers may be wholesale or retail; they may move the product to point-of-sale as quickly as possible after it is harvested, or they may hold it for several months in storage facilities where the atmosphere is controlled to retard deterioration. Processors may be located in Michigan or elsewhere; Michigan's fruit is processed into products ranging from baby food to wine.

Sooner or later the fruit reaches consumers, but its form may have changed a great deal. If it is apple juice in baby food, it may not be recognizable as an apple product. The consumers may buy the fruit directly from the farmer at a u-pick operation or roadside stand, or they may buy it at a general grocery store. They may take whatever fruit is available at the store where they buy other foods, or they may seek stores that warrant that the fruit they sell was produced without synthetic pesticides. The consumers may purchase the fruit in Michigan or other parts of the United States or in Europe or Asia or Latin America.

These five components constitute the commodity chain that sup-plies and utilizes the inputs to produce a crop that can be processed, transported, and marketed in forms that consumers desire. The other five components of the system act to strengthen or modify the links in this commodity chain. Two of these components are difficult to locate specifically. The first, research, is conducted at various places in the chain. Input agribusinesses conduct their own research on chemicals and machinery, and they contract with universities to do research for them. Land-grant universities are a major locus of research, as are other government laboratories (U.S. Department of Agriculture [USDA], Environmental Protection Agency [EPA], Food and Drug Administration [FDA]). Growers themselves conduct research on dif-ferent techniques and different cultivars. Processors support both in-house and extra mural research to determine which characteristics of the fruit can enhance their final products.

The second diffuse activity is extension, including the functions of technology transfer, education, problem solving, and leadership development. Although it is fairly easy to identify the state extension service (MSU-Extension), much extension activity goes on in other arenas. Most input suppliers have public relations programs, ranging from publications to traveling salespersons, that try to disseminate information to growers. Growers may also make arrangements to acquire certain kinds of information, even on a commercial basis, concerning markets or pest eruptions or new regulations. Producer groups seek to disseminate information to consumers about the healthfulness of apples or the sweetness of cherries.

The activities that are conducted by each of these seven components, the transactions that occur between them, and even the establishment of components like the state experiment station and cooperative extension service are governed by policies and regulations. Many of these policies are established by government bodies and agencies; while the state and federal departments of agriculture play major roles, EPA, FDA, and trade agencies are also involved. For purposes of this article we take policy to refer to any requirements or prohibitions that constrain the opportunities for activity available to other members of the system. In that perspective, policies are also made by the major marketers and processors when they specify desired or undesired characteristics in fruit, and by input suppliers when they do or do not make available certain kinds of pest management techniques.

Given the extensive scope of pest management policy, it is understandable that it becomes a highly contested terrain. While all eight of these components get involved in those contests, the ninth and tenth components also play prominent roles. The ninth component, grower associations, has already been mentioned as active in extension and research. These associations also may include only growers who operate farms, or they may also include packer-shippers and processors. In addition to elected leadership and executive staff, these associations may hire legislative representatives to present their views to legislators and other government officials.

The final component in the system is heterogeneous; it consists of all of the other interest groups who have a stake in pest management policy. During this century, these have included consumer advocacy groups, environmental interest groups, nonfarm rural residents, chemical industry groups, and international commodity traders. Since these interest groups are themselves not part of the commodity chain, they have to influence other components to implement policies reflecting their interests.

Given our view of the diffuseness of pest management policy, we would expect that policy determination occurs in many different venues, and it is not surprising that different interests try to move policy debates from one arena to another where they perceive themselves to have greater strength. Whereas early federal pest management legislation left full authority with the USDA, where agricultural chemical companies were perceived to be influential, more recent laws have shifted authority to EPA, where environmental groups are perceived to dominate. And the strength of different groups in different arenas has shifted over time; growers no longer wield the influence in state legislatures and the Congress that they did at the middle of this century.

Also, in light of the diffuse nature of pest management policy, it is not surprising that it is often ambiguous and difficult to identify; nor is it surprising that what we can identify as pest management policy lacks clear focus, is incoherent and often contradictory, and lacks any rational organization. Indeed, some analysts would argue that in the United States, and in Michigan, we do not have a pest management policy, that is: a clear set of objectives concerning pest management and a reasonably coherent set of programmatic and regulatory efforts to achieve them. As previously noted, we have chosen to regard as pest management policies the various programmatic and regulatory activities that exist, and to discuss them as such.

Current pest management policies. In particular, we wish to highlight five principal elements of current pest management policy:

- Registration of Uses
- Residue Tolerances
- Grades and Standards
- Applicator Licensing
- Research and Extension

While some of these have evolved over years of legislative action, others are more recent. While some of these have the force of federal law, others are implemented by actors in the commodity chain.

Registration of uses. The concept underlying federal pest management policy from the 1920s through the 1950s was that pesticides in the marketplace should be safe and efficacious. This concept was embodied in the regulatory practice of registering a particular substance for certain uses. A manufacturer requesting registration of a substance is required to present data showing that that substance, when applied in the recommended way, does control the targeted pest(s) and does not endanger the health of consumers. The implementation of the concept of registration has always been controversial because of protest registration and revocation. Under protest registration, if the administering agency denied a requested registration, the manufacturer could protest the denial and market the substance while the protest was being considered. For reasons we discuss in greater detail later, it was not anticipated that revocation of registration would be a common occurrence, so the law made revocation procedures very difficult; with pest resistance and improvements in residue detection, revocation is now a much more common issue.

Residue tolerances. While pesticides are developed to target certain pests, their potential impact on humans makes it necessary to develop standards for the maximum concentration of each substance that will be allowed in marketed food. A grower wants a pesticide to remain effective against the target pest as long as possible; however most pesticides gradually break down into other compounds. These several considerations come together in establishing a residue tolerance, the maximum concentration of the pesticide allowed in fruit at the point it is sold by the grower. The recommended application rate and timing are such that the effects of weather will have reduced the concentration below the tolerance by the time the fruit is marketed. While residue tolerances are part of federal pest management legislation, they can also be established by individual action; one of the major purchasers of Michigan's apples enforced a policy of zero Alar residue when federal regulations allowed its presence.

Residue tolerances as a mechanism for achieving the objective of food safety have suffered from a variety of problems. When it was first implemented, many tolerances were set "below the detectable level"; but as detection methods improved from parts per million to parts per trillion, it became necessary to do the work to identify a safe tolerance level. When the tolerance mechanism was implemented, it was assumed that the major concern was acute toxicity, which is relatively easy to ascertain. But with improvements in epidemiological techniques and in scientific understanding of cancer, birth defects, genetic disorders, and impacts on the endocrine system, concern shifted to these effects. The use of the tolerance mechanism was based on the assumption that human reaction to these substances was fairly uniform, varying largely by body weight; what was safe for one would be safe for all. But advances in clinical technology have shown that some individuals are much more sensitive than others to these substances; this has raised the issue: for which subgroup in the population should the standard be set.

After a pesticide tolerance has been established by the EPA, it is enforced for meat, poultry, and some egg products by the USDA and for all other foods in interstate commerce by the FDA. Imported foods are monitored by these two agencies. States may also establish regulations to monitor pesticide residues for food produced and sold within their boundaries;[3] Michigan enforces exactly the same residue standards as the FDA with the exception of mercury in fish, where the Michigan residue tolerance is half that of the FDA.[4] FDA's program of residue monitoring includes both sampling individual lots of foodstuffs as they pass through commercial exchange, and a total diet study that estimates the dietary intake of pesticide residues for eight age/sex groups based on marketbaskets of 234 food items sampled in four regions of the country.[5]

Other than registration and residue tolerances, no other component of pest management policy considers the risks to human and environmental health imposed by the use of pesticides. In this situation, the manufacturers and users of pesticides are able to externalize some of the true cost of pesticide use, i.e., to impose on others the costs of remedying some of the negative impacts caused by pesticides. For example, if herbicides contaminate the water supply of a municipality, it is the citizens of the city, rather than the manufacturers of the herbicide or the farmers who used it, who pay to purify the contamination or to obtain water from another source.

Grades and standards. Grades and standards apply to the size, shape, and color of the fruit. They may disallow the presence of bruises or wormholes. These standards were created to make marketing more orderly, i.e., to reduce the transaction costs of buyers and sellers by creating descriptive categories for an inherently variable product. For produce to be classified in the top categories, pest damage must be controlled. Thus, whereas residue tolerances establish a maximum for the amount of pesticide applied, grades and standards necessitate the application of at least some minimum amount of pesticide.[6] Grades and standards may be set by federal marketing orders or by private buyers. Most wholesale buyers today require higher standards than those specified by federal grades and standards. The largest purchaser of Michigan's tart cherry production has specified that there be no appearance of maggot damage. Ten years ago the Organization for Economic Cooperation and Development proposed a plan for the international standardization of fruit and vegetables.[7] This included detailed cosmetic standards for fruit and vegetables.[8] Recently the European Community has adopted the OECD standards for internal exchange and for imports; some writers have suggested that these will come to predominate in production around the world.

Applicator licensing. During the 1970s and 1980s, earlier concerns for efficacy and food safety were joined by concerns for environmental impact and worker safety. It was assumed that growers were not following the manufacturer's printed directions, were using outdated and unreliable equipment, and did not understand the potential environmental and health impacts of the pesticides. For these reasons, legislation was passed that only persons holding licenses could apply pesticides commercially. In order to receive a license, one had to attend a course and pass a test. Licenses had to be renewed every three years after attending refresher courses or passing a test for farmers in Michigan.

Research and extension. The extent of research and extension activities throughout the fruit commodity chain has been discussed. Here, we would simply note that these activities have always been supported by federal and state funds as well as money from input manufacturers and grower associations. But even these activities have not been without controversy. Some writers have noted that public support comes to resemble pork barrel or blueberry pie legislation; for years MSU received federal money in a line item for blueberry maggot research. Other writers have argued that research continues to seek more potent pesticides when more attention ought to be paid to environmental impacts and food safety issues.

SOURCES OF CHANGE IN PEST MANAGEMENT POLICY

While pest management policy has changed significantly during the past 100 years, the current situation is characterized by an unusually large array of social, economic, and political forces pushing pest management policy in several different directions. In this section we discuss nine major influences for change in pest management policy:

- Current Pest Management Policy
- International Trade
- Consumer Preferences
- Environmental Pollution
- Pest Resistance
- Land Use
- Labor Availability
- Costs of Replacement Techniques for Pest Management
- Industry Protection

Some of these forces, like the costs of developing alternative techniques and pesticide resistance, are internal to agriculture. Other forces, including trade liberalization, consumer preferences, land use practices, and government regulations, come from the social context surrounding agriculture. Still other forces, like environmental concerns and issues of sustainability, are based on the abiotic and biotic context in which agriculture is practiced. The situation is made even more complex by the fact that a force for change may push pest control in different directions. For example, consumers express preferences for low or nil pesticide residues on their fruit and for fruit with pristine appearance (which in today's plant protection systems means high pesticide inputs). While we refer to these sources of influence on pest management policy as forces for change, we want to be clear that these "forces" are the expressions of preferences of components of the system as we previously described it.

Current pest management policy. Some aspects of current pest management policy are themselves a force for change. Many current policies represent a compromise between contending viewpoints in previous deliberations. Yet those differing viewpoints continue to try to achieve their special interest goals. As we have noted in the previous section, the major special interest groups contending in pest management policy deliberations are growers, the agrichemical industry, commodity groups, and consumers and environmentalists. For example, current federal policy may allow a manufacturer to sell existing stocks of a pesticide after its registration has been revoked. This federal policy has precipitated many efforts for the removal of this exemption. The removal is very likely to be an issue again when FIFRA (the Federal Insecticide, Fungicide, and Rodenticide Act) is considered for renewal in the near future. Although federal regulations require that data on health impacts be submitted for registration, the legislation does not clearly indicate what should be done if the submitted data are later found to be unreliable. In this situation, the state of California has required new data and in 1993 suspended the registration of over 100 pesticides when their producers did not submit the results of new studies.[9]

Re-registration can be instigated either by a finding of faulty data or by new data indicating health hazards which were not considered in the original registration. In either case, as the understanding of the potential hazards of pesticides has improved, the testing necessary for re-registration has become more costly. As a result, the manufacturers of pesticides which have only a relatively small market may choose not to seek re-registration for that use for that pesticide. This has led to proposals for exemptions from testing (IR-4s) for these "minor use" pesticides. For example, Pirimor is a very selective pesticide for aphids, with no known impacts on natural enemies or other beneficial insects. Because it is a systemic insecticide, it works through the plant's system rather than on the surface, and a residue remains in the fruit; therefore a tolerance is required. Since the market for this use is very small, the manufacturer of Pirimor does not regard it as profitable to pay the cost of testing which would be required to establish a tolerance level; instead Pirimor will not be registered for that use.

Pest management policy is also affected by other federal policies on toxic substances. Recent changes in "right-to-know" and SERA TS&G III legislation mandate that police and fire officials be informed or have access to information detailing the exact identity and location of toxic chemicals stored in buildings. The same legislation also mandates that all workers, including farm workers, have access to a list of the toxic chemicals being used at their place(s) of employment and the hazards associated with each toxic substance.

International trade. Although much attention has focused recently on the potential impacts of the North American Free Trade Agreement (NAFTA), the approval of this trade agreement is actually only one of several changes in the international trade arena that will affect pest management policy. At least as important as NAFTA are the potential impacts of changes in the General Agreement on Trade and Tariffs (GATT). While the overall aim of the revisions to GATT is to establish free and open competition, one of the ways in which it does this is by proscribing direct subsidies to an industry. In the case of United States agriculture, this could have the unintended effect of reducing the use of pesticides, for the following reasons. One of the reasons pesticides are used heavily on row and field crops is to reduce damage by pathogens and insect pests, which build up in fields planted continuously in the same crop. An alternative to heavy pesticide use is crop rotations or combining crops that are not hosts to the same pests. But subsidy programs that determine their payments on the base acreage of a certain crop encourage a farm operator to maximize the base acreage and discourage the use of any land for crop rotations. If it does turn out that the changes in GATT eliminate direct subsidies, it will also eliminate one barrier to crop rotations in the United States.

At the same time that changes in GATT may decrease the motivation to use pesticides, they may also decrease the ability to control the use of pesticides. Recent decisions under the current GATT have held that a nation cannot exclude imported produce on the basis of the techniques used to produce the goods, and it is expected that these decisions will be preserved in the revisions to GATT. It was agreed in the current revisions to GATT that a nation can restrict produce imports on the basis of residues from a production technique if it is claimed that those residues are injurious to human, animal, or plant health. Although each nation can set residue standards, if the standard adopted is not one that has been internationally adopted (e.g., in Codex Alimentarius) it can be challenged under the GATT dispute resolution procedures.[10] While in principle a nation can exclude produce imports for phytosanitary contamination that poses a threat to domestic animals or plants (e.g., an exotic parasite or a resistant pest), if the exclusion is challenged, the excluding nation has to convince a technical expert group, convened under the GATT dispute settlement procedures, that the exclusion is based on a real threat that is not already present in the country's environment.[11] While the concern of GATT is with non-discrimination and transparency in international trade, it is not concerned with environmental protection or human health. Thus, while standards that are more stringent than international ones can be challenged, any nation is free to adopt residue standards that are less stringent than international ones. In doing so, that nation creates a market for foods produced in any other country using techniques that are more risky and (perhaps) less costly. This makes it possible for growers to export produce that does not meet the domestic standard for quality, pesticide residues, and/or phytosanitation to countries with less-stringent standards at a low price to the detriment of other producers who use more costly methods to grow safer produce.

If phytosanitary regulations are permitted under GATT and/or NAFTA, it is suggested that they will be used in place of tariffs as trade barriers to protect local producers. Compliance with these phytosanitary barriers is expected to result in increasing use of within-season pesticide controls and postharvest treatments to eliminate insects and pathogens in order to assure acceptance by GATT and NAFTA markets. But the two principal postharvest treatments for fruits and vegetables are methyl bromide and phosphine. Increasing use of these two treatments raises concerns because the former depletes the ozone layer and several species are now resistant to the latter. Beyond the details of within-season and postharvest treatments, increasing the strength of phytosanitary regulations also increases the barriers to biological controls. For example, lacewings (*Chrysopa spp.*) could be used to control aphids in blueberries, but some boxes of blueberries at retail stores might contain lacewing larvae, which elicit a phytosanitary rejection in some markets; if the presence of such larvae were not banned by phytosanitary regulations, growers would have the option of using lacewings instead of broad-spectrum insecticides that yield residues at harvest.

Both NAFTA and the European Community's integration explicitly seek to harmonize pesticide regulations and residue tolerances and to establish a general registration system, but the impacts of this process are difficult to anticipate. If harmonization is driven by concerns about pollution and food safety, then many pesticides that growers are accustomed to using will be banned; but if the guiding principle for harmonization is to minimize disruption of existing practices, then many growers will be able to use pesticides at rates or in formulations that were previously forbidden, and even will have available pesticide chemistries previously banned.

Consumer preferences. A third constellation of forces producing change in pest management policy arises from consumer preferences for food attributes. As noted in the discussion of current pest management policy, the market for fruit and vegetables in the United States is characterized by very high standards for external appearance. Proponents justify these cosmetic standards on the grounds that consumers demand good-looking produce. But research indicates that consumers are willing to accept tradeoffs between appearance on the one hand, and pesticide residues and environmental pollution on the other hand.[12] Further, the consumer-demand argument ignores the ways in which buyers have been taught to believe that "the only good

produce is gorgeous produce." Another argument in favor of the cosmetic standards is that the levels of pesticide use required to achieve
"gorgeous" appearance also avert the contamination of food by toxic
substances generated by pathogen or insect infestation. Determining
the validity of this argument is very important, because if growers
could find a market for fruit and vegetables with 10 percent more
damage than currently accepted, they could reduce their use of pesticides by more than 50 percent.[13]

At the same time that growers and marketers say that consumers
demand cosmetic standards, citizens also express high levels of concern about pesticide residues. When asked to rate different foods as
being safe or unsafe, respondents in a national random sample survey
of 2,800 adults in 1992[14] were significantly more likely to feel comfortable with produce on which pesticides had not been used (see
table 1).

Table 1. Food Is Grown or Raised In Unsafe Ways		
	Percentage safe	Percentage unsafe
Organically grown fruits and vegetables.	86.5	2.3
Fruit or vegetables grown using conventional pesticides, and then tested to ensure that no pesticide residues are present.	77.4	7.1
Fruits or vegetables grown using conventional pesticides, and then tested to ensure that pesticide residues are within government limits.	62.5	14.1
Fruits or vegetables grown using conventional pesticides at approved levels.	60.5	14.6

This concern with toxic substance residues hit Michigan producers
most recently in the controversy over the use of Alar on apples. It is
not our purpose in this article to assess the merits of the different sides
in that controversy. We wish merely to point out two aspects of the
controversy. First, the controversy is situated within a context where
there are no consensual standards for assessing risk and safety that are
widely supported by scientists and the general public. In that situation,

any viewpoint in the controversy can use "Madison Avenue" approaches of persuasion via the mass media to manipulate public opinion in a desired direction. Indeed, the media itself may have a particular interest in one position and present this bias through ostensibly objective reporting. Second, one consequence of that controversy has been that Michigan growers are leery of using any substance that might cause their produce to be excluded from the market, even if that substance might be preferable to other techniques on environmental or health criteria.

In the past, as was noted in the discussion on current pest management policy, public concern about the health impacts of pesticide residues has generated demands for food safety standards and inspection programs. Three alternatives to reliance on governmental standards are available to consumers. First, they may grow their own produce; national surveys suggest that almost half of United States households produce at least some of their own food in a garden.[15] Second, they may buy directly from growers who use or avoid certain practices, or they may buy from stores that enforce standards of production and/or safety. Third, they may test their food themselves; while in the past this was a remote and expensive possibility, firms are now marketing biochemical diagnostic systems to consumers to test for pesticide residues. A diagnostic system that tests 100 food samples biochemically costs about $35 and is sensitive to one part per million, whereas most pesticide residue standards are several parts per million. This gives the consumer the capability to look for produce that is below the detectable level or actually pesticide free. The results of a national survey[16] indicate that consumers are willing to pay a higher price to be certain that produce meets federal standards or is free of residues; purchasing a home diagnostic device is one way of paying a higher price. The additional cost of 35 cents per pound of produce is similar to the willingness to pay found by the national survey. One potential consequence of the widespread use of these diagnostic systems could be that growers will be motivated not to use organophosphate and carbamate insecticides and to use instead formulations that may be more harmful to the environment but are not detectable by these systems. Further, growers will be motivated not to use effective late-season tools that might leave a residue and to use instead heavier spraying earlier in the season, which may cause more damage to the environment but will have degraded beyond detectability before harvest. In any event, these impacts will vary by commodity and by agroecosystem, so the complexity belies any generalization.

Environmental pollution. At least since *Silent Spring*, conventional pest management practices have been widely viewed as a significant source of environmental pollution. For purposes of this discussion, we divide these impacts into those affecting biota, ones affecting abiotic elements of the environment, and those affecting ecosystem structure and function. Although they may not always be the most significant, impacts of pest management practices on the abiotic components of the environment receive significant attention. Any discussion of air pollution, groundwater contamination, or surface water degradation usually identifies pest management practices as one of the causes. Chlorinated hydrocarbon insecticides (e.g., DDT, DDE) eventually reached places as far away as Antarctica through atmospheric transport and biomagnification. Fumigant pesticides such as methyl bromide diminish the ozone layer. Groundwater contamination by insecticides and herbicides has become critical in places around the country. Rivers and lakes can also be contaminated by pesticides; for many years consumption of fish from Lake Michigan has been discouraged because of the accumulation in their tissues of chlorinated hydrocarbons from agricultural and residential pesticides and industrial uses.

The unintended impacts of pesticides on living creatures are divided into non-target impacts and off-target impacts. The former pertain to living things other than the target species that are killed or harmed at the site where the pesticide is applied. Doses of some herbicides at levels specified on the labels also kill the soil biota that decompose organic matter into chemical states that plants can use as nutrients; when honeybees forage in areas that have been sprayed, they pick up encapsulated pesticides and carry them back to the hive, causing high levels of mortality. Off-target impacts occur when living things are killed or harmed away from the site of application. Off-target impacts usually occur when the pesticide is carried by air or water to an unintended location; insecticides can drift from the target field or orchard and kill beneficial species including natural enemies.

Pesticides also affect systemic properties of the environment. Precisely because they are toxic chemicals, pesticides kill many species of micro- and mesoflora and fauna other than the intended pest. These non-target impacts include species whose role in the ecosystem is well understood (e.g., colembola that shred plant litter), and others whose function in the trophic structure is not well understood (e.g., many species of mycorrhyzae). The combined effect of these many impacts is to reduce the diversity of the biota in the agroecosystem; it may thus become less stable and resilient.

One example will suffice to illustrate the complexity entailed in developing pest management strategies, even considering only the environmental aspects. When environmental concern increased in the United States in the 1960s and 1970s, one focus of concern was soil erosion from agricultural land. Over the years farmers had been encouraged to keep their land clean of weeds and plant residues so that the life cycles of weeds, plant pathogens, and insect pests would be interrupted. But keeping the land clean meant many cultivations, each of which left the topsoil bare and erodible; topsoil erosion and surface water siltation were the result. In an effort to reduce soil erosion, "no-till" practices were adopted to replace cultivation with applications of herbicides both before and after the emergence of the crop. But extensive applications of herbicides resulted in non-target impacts on soil biota, groundwater pollution, and surface water pollution leading to off-target impacts. Concern for the environmental impacts of herbicides has led agronomists to seek other ways to combat pest buildup in soil and crop residues and to see some virtue in "trashy agriculture." The whole sequence has left some farmers confused and even more convinced that agricultural scientists do not know what they are talking about.

Pest resistance. While concerns about the health impacts of pest management practices have existed for almost a century, and the environmental impacts of those practices have been a focus of concern for several decades, pest resistance has been widely acknowledged as a matter of concern for less than a decade. Basic evolutionary theory predicts that exposing a population repeatedly to a toxic chemical, organism, or practice will select for individuals for whom that control tactic is not harmful, and that this will result in the development of a population that is resistant to that tactic. Nevertheless, it has been a claim of some proponents of agrichemicals that it would always be possible to develop a new pesticide for that pest. Yet, while resistance was reaching alarming dimensions, it has been more difficult to discover new insecticides and more expensive to bring them to the marketplace, in part due to novel chemistries and in part due to increased regulation. The confluence of these two trends brought the problem of pest resistance to widespread attention. The resulting investigations of pesticide resistance have shown that the genetic changes that produce resistance to one pesticide may also produce tolerance for chemically similar pesticides (cross resistance), and may even produce multiple mechanisms of resistance for dissimilar toxic chemicals (multiple resistance) in the same pest population; both of these processes result in insects, plant pathogens, and weeds referred to as "super pests."

Pest resistance currently costs United States agriculture directly and indirectly between two and four billion dollars per year. At the present time over 20 insect species, 100 plant pathogens, and 100 weed species are resistant to all registered pesticides. The numbers of resistant species are growing at 5 to 10 percent per year, depending on the phylum. In Michigan, corn production is reduced by atrazine resistant weeds, apple production is decreased by insecticide resistant leafrollers, potato yields are diminished because no currently registered pesticides remain effective against the Colorado potato beetle, and the value of ornamental production is decreased by aphids and thrips that are resistant to insecticides. As noted in the discussion of international trade and phytosanitary regulations, one of the two principal postharvest treatments for phytosanitation is no longer effective because many species have become resistant to it.

The increasing frequency of pest resistance has several major consequences. First, the loss of pesticide efficacy is usually partial rather than absolute, both because the genetic composition of the pest population changes gradually and because resistance is usually in the form of increased tolerance rather than absolute immunity (although immunity eventually does occur). So the initial response to resistance is to use the existing pesticide at higher and higher concentrations and with greater and greater frequency, which results in the health and environmental problems noted and accelerates the development of resistance. Second, pest resistance stimulates a change to newer, more expensive pesticide chemistries. Not only does this start a new cycle of resistance development, but it exacerbates the cost-price squeeze that the grower faces, thus reducing producer profits even more. Third, faced with a choice between higher costs of increased use of the existing pesticide or higher costs of the new pesticide, some producers stop producing the crop for which the resistant pest is a problem.

Fourth, resistance makes the negotiations and arrangements concerning international trade even more complex. Agreements may or may not specify whether Country A may exclude produce from

Country B if that produce is believed to carry a population or strain of a pest that is resistant to the pesticide currently or potentially in use for that pest in Country A. Even if resistance is accepted as a legitimate basis for exclusion, the two countries may not agree on the appropriate tests to determine if the resistant strain is present in the produce or whether or not it is already present in Country A. Reliable and determinative tests may involve identifications of particular DNA forms. Finally, the increasing development of pesticide resistance is generating crises of production for particular commodities in particular regions, and these crises motivate producers, processors, and marketers to look for alternatives to heavy reliance on pesticides. We will return to this impact in the next part of the article.

Land use. Several trends in land-use patterns in the United States are also forcing changes in pest management policy. While suburban expansion exacerbates conflicts over pesticide use, rising farmland values decrease the feasibility of crop rotations as a means of pest management because producers optimize economically rather than ecologically. In addition, the increasing prevalence of feedlot operations for animal production concentrates animals and their pathogens and pests, leading to increased antibiotic and pesticide use. On the other hand, policies that lead farmers to allow some of their land to remain fallow or "set aside" have been found to have benefits for wildlife and for the preservation of susceptible pest populations as well as beneficial predators and parasites.

In Michigan as in other states, the past three decades have seen increasing conflicts concerning land use in rural areas. Suburbs have expanded into rural agricultural areas, often in discontinuous "leapfrog" patterns that brought new residents seeking arcadian, pristine environments into conflict with farmers accustomed to utilizing the land for production. While the new residents sought strict enforcement of strong environmental standards, farmers countered by seeking passage of right-to-farm legislation. Because fruit and vegetable production derives advantages from locating at the rural-urban or farm-nonfarm interface, these commodities are especially susceptible to such land use conflicts. Farm location in close proximity to urban areas gives fruit and vegetable producers access to higher value markets such as u-pick, on-farm and roadside sales, farmers' markets, and direct sales to retailers.

In part, as a result of the increasing demand for rural residences, the past three decades have also seen increasing farmland values. As farmland becomes more expensive, it becomes more difficult for farmers to allow it to remain fallow or to rotate nonmarket or lower value crops on it. In this situation, government programs, such as Payment-In-Kind (PIK), cropland set-asides, and conservation reserve, which provide farmers with some compensation for the income they forego by not planting a high-value crop, can tip the balance of the farmer's calculus in favor of practices that are more beneficial for the environment. One rationale for these payments is that society benefits from the reduced pollution of the environment and the habitat that is created for wildlife. For example, one of the easiest ways to augment Michigan's deer herd and songbird and pheasant populations is to encourage rotations and fallowing. Any of the practices, such as integrated pest management or cropland set-asides (known by some as "trashy agriculture" because they do not create pristine fields), allow increased plant diversity that provides food and cover for greater numbers of, and more diverse, wildlife. Some viewers, both growers and the general public, object to "trashy agriculture" because they have been socialized to believe that clean fields are good fields; these aesthetic norms must be changed so that people can appreciate more diverse landscapes.

Just as changes in institutional systems could encourage environmentally beneficial practices, changes in the structure of costs and benefits could motivate farmers to change the physical structure of their farms in ways that increase biodiversity. Increasing the diversity of the farm environment provides refugia for several types of species. First, having areas where pests are not suppressed with current pesticides maintains susceptible genes that will slow the evolutionary pressure toward resistance. Second, having areas that are managed as habitat for beneficial species provides populations of natural enemies of crop pests that will suppress the pests before they erupt.

One particular form of land use that has significant implications for pest management is feedlot production of beef and swine. Raising any species of animals in situations of close crowding and high concentration leads to increased disease and pest problems. To deal with these problems, preventive medical treatments are mixed into the animals' feeds, but repeatedly treating a population of pathogens in this way can result in antibiotic resistance. Once a particular disease is resistant to existing antibiotics, epidemics can proliferate, and if the pathogen infects humans, these practices could impact the health of Michigan's population. Concentrating animals on feedlots also produces concentrations of animal manure, which can lead to higher fly populations. Efforts to control fly problems by incorporating insecticides in ear tags and in the feed as "feed through" controls have produced resistant strains of flies that in time may affect human populations.

Labor availability. Part of the impetus for the increased use of pesticides in Michigan agriculture has been the need for an alternative to human labor, and there is no reason to expect that pressure to diminish. The labor needed to hoe weeds and remove caterpillars has been replaced by herbicides and insecticides. In Michigan, average labor costs are high compared to other areas of the country or the world; unionization in general, and specifically in agricultural labor, has led to improved compensation and working conditions. If food is to be produced cheaply, chemical inputs are less expensive than hired labor, especially if the environmental and health costs of those chemical inputs can be externalized outside agriculture.

As noted in the description of the agricultural system, the labor that is still needed for farm production is supplied by members of the farm family, hired laborers, and service contracts. Recent farm labor legislation has increased the standards for worker safety; farm workers must be informed when a pesticide has been applied in a field where they are working, and a waiting period before workers can enter the field is mandated.[17] Also under the worker right-to-know legislation, farm workers must be told what chemicals are stored or have been used, and what are their potential effects.

As pesticide applicator licensing becomes more stringent, more and more growers will rely on contract services to apply their pesticides. At the moment very little is known about the optimal size of these firms or about their linkages with pesticide manufacturers or grower associations. As they develop, these professional applicators will become a force for change.

Costs of replacement techniques for pest management. In general, compared to their predecessors, the costs of new pest management techniques are even greater than would be expected from the rate of inflation. In the case of pesticides, this is partly because the costs of research and development rise as resistance develops to more families of chemicals. It is also partly because newer pesticides are narrower in scope, less toxic, and less persistent than older ones, and chemicals with these properties are more difficult to discover or synthesize. And, it is due to the patentability of synthesized compounds; the developing firm can seek to maximize the return on its investment during the lifetime of the patent.

Biological control techniques are also in general more expensive than recent chemical techniques, in part because the testing procedures for certification of these techniques are more complex; introduced diseases and exotic predators must be shown to have no unintended consequences. The major exception to this generalization is the propagation and release of natural enemies; because these methods do not require certification, they can be developed at lower cost. For the reasons noted, crop rotations are also, in general, more expensive than chemical treatments. To maintain the volume of production, additional land must be rented or purchased; different machinery must be bought or contracted for the rotation crop; and, in general, markets for rotation crops (e.g., grass hay) are either poor or non-existent.

Because they substitute information-gathering and decisionmaking for single-factor methods, integrated pest management (IPM) techniques are even more expensive than their chemical and biological components. IPM techniques require professional personnel to monitor and interpret the climatic factors used to forecast pest outbreaks. Growers themselves need additional education, often provided by IPM schools, to understand the IPM approach and monitor pest and predator levels. Pest management professionals require training in the use of the new techniques.

Industry protection. Just as pests have evolved in ways that protect their species, the pest control industry has also evolved in ways that protect its markets. We have noted the use of patents to maximize profits on synthesized chemicals; as chemical companies have moved into the co-development of crop varieties and pesticides (designer chemicals), patents have been granted on the new varieties also. In some cases to protect the biological information, no patent is sought, and the information remains proprietary. This has raised concerns about the potential for economic concentration in the production of seeds and pesticides for certain types of crops, and the need for antitrust activity in this area.

Compared to other inputs to farm production, the pesticide industry has always enjoyed a somewhat privileged position; pesticide salespersons know much more about pesticides than most farmers, and this disparity in knowledge is much greater for pesticides than for seed or machinery or land inputs. For this reason, pesticide salespersons are significant purveyors of information, but their position is inherently conflicted. To sell their product they must emphasize the potential threats posed by the pest and the extent to which their product can protect against those threats. It is not always in their interest to provide an objective assessment of the threat, or to balance the cost of the threat against the negative impacts of the pesticide, even the long-run diminution of the efficacy of the pesticide itself. Some pesticide salespersons do adopt a position which emphasizes the short-run interest of the farmer rather than the interest of the company, but even then their advice adheres firmly to the chemical model of farming.

Alternative policy responses. With this diverse set of forces pushing pest management policy in several directions at the same time, we suggest that the time is opportune for more explicit attention to pest management policy questions. One of the reasons that it is so difficult to see where pest management policy is headed is precisely because it is largely derivative of other policy issues, as we have indicated in the previous section. Thus, for example, pest management policy is, to a large extent, determined by food safety regulations, international trade agreements, and crop support programs, rather than considerations of optimal pest management. We suggest that the current situation provides an opportunity to approach the question of pest management policy proactively, and that the likely approaches might be grouped under the following rubrics.

One approach to pest management represents a continuation of the current trajectory, and as such, it implies that the conflict between the forces of change described in the previous section will continue and increase. In this approach, pesticide manufacturers will continue to develop new pesticides, environmental agencies will continue to tighten environmental regulations, and food agencies will continue to strengthen food safety regulations. This approach is largely reactive, responding to each problem of environmental contamination or pesticide resistance or health risk as it occurs. While these responses may be innovative, they represent, at best, efforts to muddle through rather than to optimize. One set of innovations consists of biotechnological solutions, such as transgenic species which displace pests by competition; the wisdom of this approach is currently under debate, and no transgenic species have been registered for use in pest management. Another set of innovations are the so-called "biorational pesticides" which use naturally occurring substances to interfere with the pests' natural processes; these include pheromone disrupters to interfere with mating, hormone growth regulators to interfere with growth, and other natural products which are toxic to the pests. While this approach points away from artificial chemicals and toward substances that occur naturally, and while it points in the direction of alternative pest control strategies, it remains reactive and muddling rather than forward-looking and optimizing; in particular, it does not solve the problems of residues on, and toxins in, food.

The second set of approaches to pest management emphasizes future-oriented planning and development taking into account the forces for change. These approaches minimize the occurrence of pesticide resistance by using pest control measures at the lowest effective levels. They minimize environmental pollution by making explicit the total cost of cosmetic appearance standards. They minimize health risks by relying as much as possible on predator controls and naturally occurring substances. Most important, these approaches view pest management policy as a way of directing change in the human ecosystem. In this view, the role of policy is to plan for the likely effects of current activities; for example, if a decision is made to import apples from Country A, then the search can begin now for a natural predator for the exotic pests that are likely to be brought in with that fruit. These approaches are also proactive in creating refugia for non-resistant pest populations and in providing compensation for the benefits generated for society by farmers' decisions to create insect barriers or refugia for predators, to rotate crops, or to fallow land. While no single objective is maximized, all relevant criteria are considered in developing pest management policy.

If neither of these approaches is chosen, the alternative is chaos and crisis management. While this might not seem unlike the current situation, the conflicting forces for change might make things even more chaotic. What makes an international trade provision or a health risk scare so disruptive is that they are so unpredictable; at the stroke of a pen or the broadcast of a television show, a grower's fruit or vegetable crop becomes almost worthless. If no effort is made to anticipate where pollution may occur, then a grower's use of a pesticide may be suddenly interrupted when a government agency finds contamination in the course of a water quality screening.

RECOMMENDATIONS FOR POLICY CHANGES

For the reasons indicated in the previous section, we feel strongly that future-oriented planning and development of pest management policy is the best of the three alternatives. We believe that efforts to continue along the current trajectory, even with new technologies, will eventually become too costly in human and physical resources. In addition, we believe that chaos and crisis management imposes too great a cost on the growers, consumers, and citizens who cannot protect themselves against the risks. A core component of future oriented planning is integrated pest management. Rather than focusing on one particular approach to pest management, IPM starts with the premise that the many different approaches all have a role to play in pest management and that the optimal strategy is to identify the proper role for each technique. IPM is not chemical; it is not organic; it is not biological—it is all of those things. For this reason, we refer to it as the middle road in pest management policy. In this section, we describe a pest management policy based on IPM, suggest what implications this would have for public agencies, and indicate the needs for information and technology.

IPM—the middle road of pest management. No fewer than three of the last six presidents of the United States have made commitments to integrated pest management (IPM). The Clinton administration like the Carter and Nixon administrations have identified IPM as a component of their comprehensive pesticide policy. However, in an unprecedented move, the current administration called for 75 percent implementation of IPM on America's crop land by 2000.[18] Why after twenty-one years are politicians still calling for IPM implementation?

Part of the reason is that IPM has evolved over time. Initially it stood for the integration of economic injury levels, natural controls, chemicals, and biological controls into a set of management strategies that could limit pests with minimum adverse affects on the environment and society. Early on IPM implementors discovered that this was extremely challenging to do, and implementation slowed to a crawl. The barriers to IPM implementation included obstacles in the adoption process, lack of workable IPM systems, the dynamics of agricultural agroecosystems, lack of well-trained and experienced personnel, and a failure of institutions to sustain funding beyond the first implementation phases. In the intermediate years, IPM came to mean almost any reduction in pesticide use including reduced rates, reduced

frequency of sprays, and better timing through monitoring and pre-
diction systems. Even switching to selective or less environmentally-
damaging chemistry was viewed as IPM. Under this modified IPM
definition the agrichemical industry embraced many IPM programs
and these programs were institutionalized into agribusiness in the
United States.

Today the definition of IPM is again changing, returning to its earlier meaning (i.e., maximizing natural controls) with the inclusion of
more sustainable tactics including cycling control agents (biological
control), reducing nonrenewable pest control inputs (pesticides) and
preventing pest population development through agroecosystem
design. In addition, it seeks to encompass tactics that will prevent or
slow down the development of genetic resistance by managing selection pressure on pest populations. This is the type of IPM to which the
president was referring in his address to the House of Representatives
in September 1993.

Thus current pest management policy will be changed by a commitment to focus efforts "on reducing the overall risk from the use of pesticides." To accomplish this policy, biological control agents and
biological pesticides will require unique regulatory treatment, according to Environmental Protection Agency Chief Administrator Carol
Browner. Richard Rominger, Deputy Secretary, USDA, stated that biological control for major plant pests and weed problems will continue
to be the focus of the USDA. Mr. Rominger further defined IPM from
the Clinton administration's view as, "systems . . . based on extensive
collection and interpretation of field level data to determine pest
infestation thresholds, protect non-target and beneficial species, utilize predators and parasites, and rely on synthetic pesticide use only as
a last resort."[19]

Implications for pest management policy. This policy approach would
have far reaching effects on Michigan pest management practices if it
were implemented as the Clinton administration desires before 2000.
Michigan already has a very strong IPM history since many of the
concepts and developments were pioneered at Michigan State
University. However, the support for IPM in the state has steadily
eroded to the point where there are only fragments of the previous
IPM program today. Thus, implementation on the scale called for by
the president would be impossible without major investment by federal, state, and local governments and producers. The marketing, processing, and packing/shipping sectors would also have to contribute

significantly. IPM implementation requires extensive personnel, research, and policy support across institutions like Michigan State University and key state departments including Michigan Department of Agriculture, Department of Natural Resources, and others, particularly those dealing with transportation, trade, and small business. In addition, the federal Soil Conservation Service has been supporting various IPM implementation scouting services throughout the state. These programs have generally been carried out through cooperation with Michigan State University and the MSU Extension Service.

Several additional state policy tools could also help to implement IPM in Michigan's very diverse agriculture. First, cosmetic standards and pest infestation laws could be reviewed and relaxed or changed where pest pressure has relaxed or where modern pest control programs eliminate the need for these limitations. Facilitation of trade opportunities, particularly where NAFTA is concerned, could encourage transition to IPM where these practices ensure better control of quarantinable pests. Where pesticide applicator training is already implemented through the Michigan Department of Agriculture, additional IPM training could be added on as a natural continuation of pest management information transfer.

In instances where consumer standards and environmental concern conflict (phytosanitation versus reduction of pesticide use), the various state departments, Michigan State University, private interest groups, farm workers, consumers, and environmental representatives could proceed through a conflict resolution process with the goal of jointly sponsoring programs that resolve key issues. Because effective solutions will involve internalizing the costs which currently are externalized, there may be few solutions that can be implemented at little or no cost. Nevertheless, we return to the evidence (previously cited) of consumers' willingness to pay more for food produced in ways that minimize risks to human and environmental health, and suggest that the "public goods" of reduced health risks be paid for with public monies, in the form of higher prices and/or general taxes for research and extension. And we would emphasize that just as it is important that food produced domestically not create risks to human and environmental health, it is equally important that food produced abroad for consumption in the United States not be produced in ways which pose risks to human and environmental health in the producing countries. The resolution of these issues will not be accomplished in one or two years; we expect that the process will extend over decades. Next we suggest one way in which this process might be initiated.

The Agricultural Experiment Station (AES) at Michigan State University has supported IPM research broadly for twenty years. However, this support has been far short of that required to develop the pesticide alternatives necessary to reach the Clinton administration's IPM goal. Since Michigan has the third most diverse agriculture in the U.S., the call for pesticide alternatives exceeds the AES's current IPM capacity by ten-to-twenty-fold. Furthermore, the level of maintenance research required to sustain an IPM system in the face of dynamic agroecosystems rebounding from the population suppression effects of broad spectrum pesticides is like trying to plug holes in a window screen. In time, the programs called for could be accomplished, but not without far reaching commitments in many public and private sectors.

Needs for information and technology. The middle road in Michigan pest management is a very ambitious road; we do not currently have all the vehicles and maps we need to travel this road. In this section we highlight the kinds of information and organization that are needed. We do not mean to imply, however, that all of the necessary physical, chemical, and biological technology is available. Indeed, we would give high priority to the development of IPM techniques for the period of transition away from high pesticide usage. However, since the needs for these kinds of techniques are discussed extensively elsewhere,[20] we focus our discussion on the organization and information technologies.

We noted earlier that the approaches of the middle road rely heavily on information, both about the present and the future, to make decisions about optimal pest management practices at a particular place and time. This includes information about accumulated precipitation and accumulated heat (degree-days) to forecast pest eruptions; this information needs to be specific to areal units smaller than counties. It also includes information about levels of pest populations gained from field-level monitoring. The need for these kinds of information specific to relatively small areas raises questions about how best to organize the provision of this information and its application to pest management decisions. One possibility is for MSU Extension to collect the climate data, contract for the pest monitoring, and make pest management recommendations to growers. Another possibility is for private consultants to do all of those things, with the growers who purchase the recommendations paying a fee for the service. A third possibility is to encourage the formation of pest management districts (like drainage districts) where all growers who benefit from a service are assessed for the provision of that service.

Forecasting pest eruptions pertains to making operational decisions; what should a particular grower do at a certain time on a specific field. Other kinds of information are needed about the agroecosystem itself, to construct the decisionmaking rules for the operational decisions. This systemic information includes degree of resistance among pest populations. It includes population levels of pest predators and incidence of pest pathogens. It also includes likely levels of production in future years; resistance is less of a concern if a pest is on a declining crop than if it is on an expanding crop. Again, the need for this kind of information also raises questions about how best to organize its collection and analysis. One possibility is for the Agricultural Experiment Station to support continuing projects in this area. Another possibility is for fruit producers to collect a surcharge of a certain amount or a certain percentage per bushel to create a fund to support this scientific activity; other commodities do this for advertising and market development. However, currently low levels of profit in fruit production diminish the feasibility of a contribution by growers, and the increasing competitiveness of the fruit market decreases the feasibility of raising prices to support the surcharge. If the financial support for the information service cannot come from growers, an alternative is for the State to support it, perhaps through the Department of Agriculture or MSU Extension; since the health and environmental benefits generated by changes in pest management policy are public goods, it is appropriate that the changes be publicly funded.

The importance of informational and organizational technologies, as well as developments from the physical and biological sciences, points to the need for research which looks at pest management in the context of the food system as a whole. Pest management policies themselves are established by political, social, and economic processes, and research is needed to understand the ways in which those policy determination processes operate. Many of the sources of change in pest management policy can be thought of as ethical claims for certain kinds of policies (e.g., for the economic sustainability of the farm family, for the health of the farm laborer, for the preservation of biodiversity); this suggests that the ethical aspects of pest management policy merit investigation.

These are the kinds of questions that Michigan pest management policy needs to answer in the years ahead. Arriving at effective answers will require the participation of all parties with significant interests in the questions. These include the growers, the agrichemical producers and suppliers and the farm laborers, the packer/shippers and the processors, environmental groups, food safety and consumer groups, agricultural scientists, and government officials. Establishing effective pest management policy will require more than just a workshop or a conference; part of what will make pest management policy effective is that it will be based on the ongoing involvement of these interested groups. It is the longterm commitment to the process of identifying effective policies and the research needed to implement them that will avert episodic spurts of fad research.[21] If balanced and collaborative involvement of these groups can be accomplished, so that each group feels that its viewpoint is being given effective voice, successful policies will follow.[22]

NOTES

1. Jim Flore, et al., *Report on Fruit Type of Farming in Michigan*, Michigan Agricultural Experiment Station Research Report No. 524 (East Lansing: Michigan State University Agricultural Experiment Station, 1992).
2. William H. Friedland, et al., *Manufacturing Green Gold* (Cambridge: Cambridge University Press, 1981).
3. U.S. Environmental Protection Agency, *EPA's Pesticide Programs*, Office of Pesticides and Toxic Substances, Publication Number 21T-1005 (Washington, D.C.: Government Printing Office, May 1991).
4. Personal communication, David Wade, Michigan Department of Agriculture, Pesticide and Plant Pest Management Division, 29 March 1994.
5. U.S. Food and Drug Administration, *Residue Monitoring 1991*, Division of Contaminants Chemistry (Washington, D.C.: Government Printing Office, 1992).
6. U.S. Department of Agriculture Economic Research Service-NASS, *Federal Grade Standards for Fresh Produce: Linkages to Pesticide Use*, USDA (AIB-675) (Washington, D.C.: Government Printing Office, 1993).
7. Organization for Economic Cooperation and Development, *The OCDE Scheme for the Application of International Standards for Fruit and Vegetables* (Paris: Organization for Economic Cooperation and Development, 1983).
8. Organization for Economic Cooperation and Development, *Tomatoes* (Paris: Organization for Economic Cooperation and Development, 1988).
9. State of California, Department of Pesticide Regulation, Registration Branch, *March 1993 Status Report AB 1742 Chemicals* (Sacramento: State of California, 1993).

10. GATT Secretariat, *Understanding the Proposed GATT Agreement on Sanitary and Phytosanitary Measures* (Geneva: GATT Secretariat, April 1993).

11. Personal communication, Sharon Bylenga, Office of Agricultural Affairs, Foreign Agricultural Service, 31 March 1994.

12. David Bunn, et al., "Consumer Acceptance of Cosmetically Imperfect Produce," *The Journal of Consumer Affairs* 24, no. 2 (1990):268-79; James Hammit, *Organic Carrots: Consumer Willingness to Pay to Reduce Food Borne Risks*, Report r-3447-EPA (Santa Monica: The Rand Corporation, 1986); Eileen Van Ravenswaay and John P. Hoehn, *Consumer Willingness to Pay for Reducing Pesticide Residues in Food: Results of a Nationwide Survey*, Department of Agricultural Economics Staff Paper No. 91-18 (East Lansing: Michigan State University, Department of Agricultural Economics, 1991).

13. Evaluating this possibility under current conditions is made difficult by the fact that the internalized costs of pest management are a small fraction of the grower's total cost of production. Thus even reducing pesticide costs by half does not reduce the grower's selling price significantly. So even if consumers were willing to consume blemished produce and growers brought blemished produce to market, consumers would confront a situation where the price differential between "beautiful" produce and "blemished" produce was negligible, and they would buy the "beautiful" produce in preference to the blemished. Thus, in the current situation, it is only when shortages of the beautiful commodity and its substitutes exist that blemished produce will be consumed.

14. Ronald C. Wimberley, et al., eds., *Farming and the Environment* (Boulder, Colorado: Westview Press, in press).

15. American Gardening Association, *National Survey Results* (Vermont: American Gardening Association, 1981).

16. Van Ravenswaay and Hoehn, *Consumer Willingness.*

17. U.S. Environmental Protection Agency, *The Worker Protection Standard for Agricultural Pesticides—How to Comply—What Employers Need to Know* (Washington, D.C.: U.S. Government Printing Office, 1993); Jack L. Runyan, *A Summary of the Worker Protection Standard for Agricultural Pesticides*, U.S. Department of Agriculture Economic Research Service Agriculture Information Bull. No. 680 (Washington, D.C.: Government Printing Office, 1993).

18. Testimony of officials of the U.S. Department of Agriculture, Environmental Protection Agency, and Food and Drug Administration to a joint meeting of House and Senate committees dealing with pesticides, 22 September 1993, cited in *American Journal of Alternative Agriculture* 8, no. 3 (summer 1993):139.

19. Committee on Government Operations, U.S. House of Representatives, 29 October 1993.

20. Council on Agricultural Science and Technology, *Biological Pest Control in Agriculture: Opportunities and Challenges* (Urbana: Council on Agricultural Science and Technology, in press).

21. The periodic nature of the population process of some pests generates a complementary cyclic pattern in pest management funding. After several years of dormancy, the organism which transmits X-disease erupts in year

6. The organism overwinters in the orchard, and causes damage in year 7. This generates support from commodity groups and other actors in the agricultural system for research and control measures in years 7 and 8. But little X-disease damage is seen in year 8, because of the periodic nature of the disease, so control measures are halted after a year of what might be called "revenge spraying." Also, support for research wanes, so the industry is not prepared for the next phase of the cycle, when eruption occurs in year 13. Since this cyclic pattern of funding occurs in different commodities in different states, no long-term program of research is established, even though a national or regional program would provide significant benefit to the industry.

22. The authors would like to thank Lawrence Busch, Brendan Mullan, Mike Thomas and Eileen Van Ravenswaay for the helpful comments on earlier drafts of this paper. Our work on this paper has been supported in part by the resources of the Michigan Agricultural Experiment Station. Any correspondence concerning this paper can be sent to Craig K. Harris, Department of Sociology, 429B Berkey Hall, Michigan State University, East Lansing, Michigan, 48824-1111.

SUGGESTIONS FOR FURTHER READING

Bird, George W. (1987). "Alternative Futures of Agricultural Pest Management." *American Journal of Alternative Agriculture.* 2(1): 25-29.

French, Hilary F. (1993). "Reconciling Trade and the Environment". In *State of the World 1993,* edited by Lester R. Brown, et al., 158-79. New York: W. W. Norton and Company.

National Research Council Board on Agriculture Committee on Scientific and Regulatory Issues Underlying Pesticide Use Patterns and Agricultural Innovation. (1986). *Pesticide Resistance: Strategies and Tactics for Management.* Washington, D.C.: National Academy Press.

National Research Council Board on Agriculture Committee on Scientific and Regulatory Issues Underlying Pesticide Use Patterns and Agricultural Innovation. (1986). *Pesticides and Groundwater Quality.* Washington, D.C.: National Academy Press.

National Research Council Board on Agriculture Committee on Scientific and Regulatory Issues Underlying Pesticide Use Patterns and Agricultural Innovation. (1987). *Regulating Pesticides In Foods.* Washington, D.C.: National Academy Press.

Pesticide Subcommittee of the Governor's Cabinet Council. (1985). *A Strategy for Improved Pesticide Management In Michigan.* Lansing: Michigan Department of Agriculture.

Van Ravenswaay, Eileen, et al. (1992). *Michigan Consumers' Perceptions of Pesticide Residues in Food.* Michigan State University Department of Agricultural Economics Staff Paper No. 92-56. East Lansing: Michigan State University, Department of Agricultural Economics.

Policy Issues as They Relate to the Impacts of the Gypsy Moth in Michigan

Bryan C. Pijanowski, Stuart H. Gage
and Deborah G. McCullough

STATEMENT OF PROBLEM

The gypsy moth is an introduced forest pest that consumes the leaves and needles of over 300 woody plants. Unlike many native forest insects, the gypsy moth affects urban areas as well as forested land-scapes. In great numbers, the large, hairy caterpillars create abundant frass (fecal material) and cause loss of leaves on shade and ornamental trees in wooded residential and recreational areas.

The insect was first discovered in the state forty years ago[1] and out-breaks of the pest have been occurring in Michigan since the mid-1980s. Severe defoliation (i.e., loss of leaves) of oaks, aspens, and other species preferred by gypsy moth caterpillars has occurred throughout the northern Lower Peninsula. To date, populations of gypsy moths continue to expand into southern Michigan and the Upper Peninsula. Defoliation has increased from 2,800 hectares in 1984[2] to over 280,000 hectares in 1992.[3]

In this article, we present the gypsy moth situation in Michigan as a case study of an environmental issue with widespread impacts. The history of gypsy moth management in Michigan has been affected by consideration of environmental, economic, and human health concerns and has resulted in the development of unique policies and education programs. In addition, because the gypsy moth has affected federal, state, and privately-owned forests, communication and cooperation among managers of these areas has been an important element in gypsy moth management over the years. Here, we develop a framework and identify critical elements of policies related to gypsy moth management that can be extended to similar environmental problems. Key issues identified in the Michigan gypsy moth situation include the consideration of:

1. How can we evaluate the status of gypsy moth populations and their potential impact on forests, tourism, urban areas, and other sectors?
2. Should gypsy moth population levels be controlled and what are the acceptable levels?
3. What elements are needed for an effective management program of a forest pest?

RELEVANT BIOLOGICAL AND HISTORICAL INFORMATION

How it was introduced. The gypsy moth was accidentally introduced from Europe into the Boston, Massachusetts area in 1869 by an amateur entomologist hoping to breed an "improved" silkworm.[4] Since then, the moth has expanded its range along the East Coast from Maine to North Carolina, and into the North Central region of the United States. Michigan, Ohio, Pennsylvania, West Virginia, North Carolina, and Virginia currently contain the largest populations of gypsy moths in the United States.[5] The gypsy moth has also been accidentally introduced into areas along the Pacific coast, in the states of California, Oregon, Utah, and Washington, although these western populations tend to be localized. Localized infestations and eradication programs are currently ongoing in Wisconsin, Minnesota, Illinois, Arkansas, Iowa, and Indiana.

Important life cycle information on the gypsy moth. Gypsy moth eggs are laid in masses with up to 1,200 eggs per mass. Egg masses are usually laid on tree stems or in protected places such as bark flaps, under rocks—even on the underside of lawn furniture, trailers, and wheel wells. The eggs hatch in the early spring (around the first week in May in southern Michigan) and the larvae, about 2 millimeters in length, crawl up the trunks and into the tree canopy. Larvae feed on leaves for about six weeks. They progress through several growth stages, called instars, each much larger than the former. The last instar is the most damaging. It can attain a length of 6 centimeters. During the entire larval period (instars 1-6), one caterpillar can eat as much as 1 square meter of leaves. As many as 1-2 million larvae can occupy a one acre stand of oak or aspen forest.

During mid-July the larvae encase themselves in a hardened structure called a pupal case. Here, they develop into the adult moths. Adults emerge from this casing after about 2 weeks. The adults will live only a few days, during which they mate and lay eggs. Females are unable to fly and must attract the male by emitting a chemical called a sex pheromone (i.e., a biological "perfume"). Eggs laid during one summer will hatch the following spring.

Many trees send out a new set of leaves if they lose more than 50 percent of their leaves. However, if individual trees are defoliated by gypsy moths for more than 3-5 years, they may die. In addition, tree mortality rates increase when other stress events occur, such as drought.

Spread of the gypsy moth. There are two primary means of gypsy moth dispersal into uninfested areas. First instar larvae produce a long string of silk and can be blown about by wind currents and updrafts to a maximum distance of about 20 kilometers.[6] This behavior provides a means for short range dispersal of larvae. However, humans are the main long-range dispersal agent of gypsy moths. Egg masses on vehicles, recreational equipment, firewood, and other materials are often inadvertently moved long distances, resulting in the accidental introduction of gypsy moths into uninfested areas.

History of population distributions and defoliation. Figure 1 shows the extent of the gypsy moth population distribution and abundance for the years 1985 through 1992 in Michigan. The areal extent of colonizing populations (determined as 1-200 moths per trap per year) and the size of outbreak populations (those traps having more than 200 moths per trap per year) have grown considerably over the last seven years.

These data show several interesting trends. First, populations of the gypsy moth continue to move northward into the Upper Peninsula, an

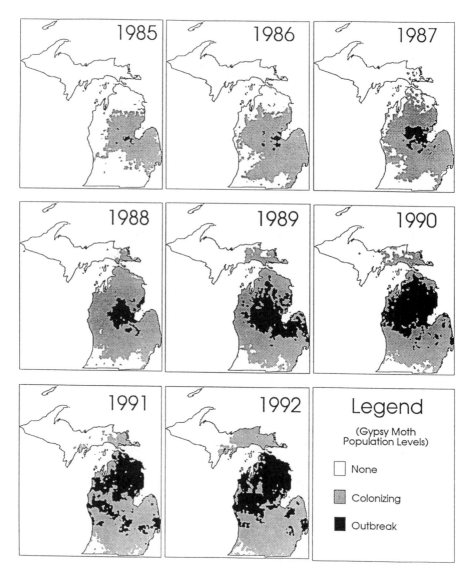

Figure 1.
Distribution and abundance of gypsy moths in the state from 1985 to 1992 as obtained through the statewide pheromone male moth trap monitoring system conducted by the Michigan Department of Agriculture and as processed in a geographic information system by the Entomology Spatial Analysis Laboratory at Michigan State University.

area that depends largely on tourism and forest products (lumber, pulp) for its income. Second, the population is continuing to expand into the highly populated urban areas of Oakland and Macomb counties. Third, populations are also expanding into the pristine Allegan State Game Refuge in the southwestern portion of Michigan, an area which contains some of the most valuable oak forests in the Lower Peninsula.

Michigan has a considerable amount of susceptible forests.[7] Estimates suggest that nearly 5.3 million hectares of forests are at risk of defoliation by gypsy moths (figure 2). Defoliation has spread from a very localized area in the center of Lower Michigan in 1984 to as far north as Cheboygan county and as far south as Allegan county in 1992 (figure 3).

Figure 2.
Location of the state's most susceptible forests (deciduous hardwoods).

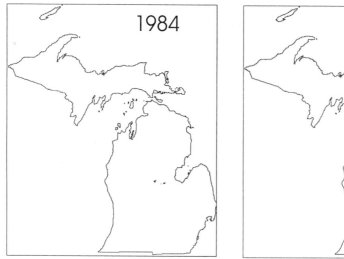 

Figure 3.
Locations of defoliation as recorded by the Department of Natural Resources in 1984 (a) and in 1992 (b).

Gypsy moth populations in forests dominated by oak, aspen or other preferred species may remain high for 2-8 years. A virus disease, combined with starvation, will eventually cause gypsy moth populations to collapse to low levels. Natural enemies such as predators (birds, mice, ants, and other predatory insects) and insect parasites will keep populations low for several years after which populations will grow again. This bimodal pattern will repeat itself, eventually developing into population cycles.

HISTORY AND PAST INITIATIVES IN MICHIGAN

Most of the effort in the 1950s and 1960s was focused on eradicating gypsy moths using DDT.[8] The goal of eradication is to eliminate the organism entirely from a geographic area. In the early 1960s it was found that DDT caused severe environmental and human health problems, and its widespread use was halted. Gypsy moth populations were monitored from 1962 through 1972 using pheromone traps baited with Gyplure, a synthetic mimic of the chemical secreted by female moths to attract males. No males were trapped, indicating that gypsy moth populations had been successfully eradicated. However, Glypure was found to be ineffective in 1972 and it was replaced with Disparlure, an improved blend of chemicals. In 1973 gypsy moths were found to be present in twenty-one counties.[9]

In 1973 the Michigan Department of Agriculture (MDA) was given permission to use carbaryl (a broad spectrum insecticide known under the trade name of Sevin which was known to be highly toxic to bees) to combat this pest. Many environmental organizations, including the Michigan Pesticides Council, the West Michigan Environmental Action Council, and the Audubon Society, criticized the use of this chemical because of a lack of knowledge regarding its effects on human health and on the environment. In addition, honey bee farmers also voiced concern that many of their bees were killed in areas that were sprayed with this chemical. Despite these concerns over its use, the Michigan Environmental Review Board (MERB) approved in 1975 the MDA's and USDA's proposal to apply Sevin in areas highly infested with gypsy moths. Subsequent application of Sevin in several counties that contained high levels of gypsy moth populations occurred in 1975.

In 1976 a new chemical, diflurobenzuron (also known as dimilin), was used instead of Sevin. Diflurobenzuron interferes with the molting process of immature insects, as well as other animals, such as crayfish, that must molt. An injunction was filed in Ingham County Circuit Court in 1978 by a group of organic farmers in central lower Michigan who were concerned that nearby use of dimilin to control gypsy moths would affect their crops. This injunction was upheld by the court and areas of gypsy moth infestations in Clare, Isabella, Mecosta, Montcalm and Saginaw counties were not treated with dimilin in 1979 and 1980. In 1981 the MDA decided to halt the use of dimilin to control gypsy moth in Michigan. Between 1972 and 1981 more than 142,000 acres of trees were treated with Sevin and dimilin by state and federal agencies.[10]

In 1983 the state of Michigan declared several counties to be "generally infested" and changed its policy from eradication to suppression of gypsy moths in wooded residential areas only. This change had several implications for the state. For example, acceptance of general infestation meant that state and federal laws would require transport regulation of plant material, such as nursery stocks, sawlogs, pulp sticks, and Christmas trees, from infested counties to uninfested counties and uninfested states.

In 1985 the MDA and Michigan Department of Natural Resources (MDNR) established a large scale, systematic trapping system for monitoring the gypsy moth distributions in the entire state (figure 4) after a design established by Gage and Mispagel.[11] This monitoring system has been conducted annually since 1985 and today represents one of the largest and most comprehensive monitoring systems on the distribution and abundance of any organism in the world. These data also are being used to determine what areas in the state should be aerially surveyed for defoliation by the MDNR, what areas should be targeted for educational activities and public meetings and also are incorporated into Michigan State University's Extension Gypsy Moth Education Bulletins.

Because of the large amount of defoliation in central lower Michigan, citizens in Isabella and Midland counties petitioned the State for relief in 1985. This petition led to the establishment in 1986 of the Michigan Gypsy Moth Suppression Program, administered by the MDA with financial support from the USDA Forest Service. This program's objective is to provide support to local governments to control the pest by spraying, by plane or helicopter, a microbial (disease causing) insecticide called *Bacillus thuringiensis* (more commonly known as *Bt*), and by introducing parasites of the pest into infested areas. Areas that can be included in treatment must meet requirements such as a minimum percentage (50 percent) of canopy cover of preferred species, expected defoliation to occur in areas of multiple homes, no potential impacts on threatened or endangered species in the vicinity, and an agreement of all property owners within spray blocks to be treated. In 1993 thirty-three counties participated in the Voluntary Suppression Program. Over 90 percent of the 250,000 acres sprayed were in privately owned, forested residential areas.[12]

The use of *Bt* to suppress the gypsy moth has also been a significant policy change made in recent years. *Bt* is considered a "safe" microbial insecticide because it is not harmful to humans or other animals such as fish or aquatic invertebrates even in high doses. Since it can be applied aerially, it is cost effective for large areas. *Bt* affects only the foliage feeding caterpillars of lepidopterans and decomposes by sunlight in a few days after application. Slightly different varieties of *Bt* have been developed to combat other pests, such as the Colorado Potato Beetle and mosquitoes.

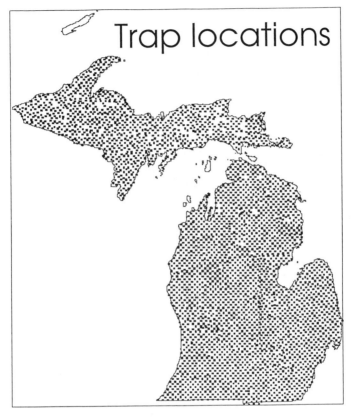

Figure 4.
Locations of the 3,108 permanent pheromone male moth traps (1 trap/18 mi²). Two traps are placed in each of Michigan's townships. Traps are monitored by the Michigan Department of Agriculture each year.

As part of the Michigan Gypsy Moth Suppression Program, an Environmental Assessment is prepared each year by the MDA and the regional USDA-Forest Service to identify: (1) areas that should be contained in the Michigan Suppression Program; and (2) the potential impact this program could have on the environment and human health. This Environmental Assessment is conducted as a requirement of the National Environmental Policy Act (NEPA) of 1969 (P.L. 91-190, 42 USC 4321). If the results of the Environmental Assessment show no impact on the environment and human health, a Finding of No Significant Impact (FONSI) statement is prepared by the USDA-FS regional office. From the Environmental Assessment, one of the management strategies contained within is also chosen by the USDA-FS with reasons cited in a statement referred to as a Decision Notice (a decision on what management alternative should be selected). However, if one of the management alternatives in the Environmental Assessment predicts an environmental impact and a decision is made to go with this alternative in the Decision Notice, then an Environmental Impact Statement (EIS) must be developed as required by the Environmental Protection Agency. A Steering Committee comprised of representatives from MDA, MDNR, Michigan State University (MSU), MSU-Extension, and county personnel meets periodically to review policies and issues related to the Voluntary Suppression Program.

ACTORS AND INSTITUTIONS

There have been a wide variety of institutions involved in addressing the gypsy moth problem in Michigan. The key players, and their roles, include the following.

United States Department of Agriculture-Animal Health Inspection Service. The USDA-APHIS is responsible for detection trapping ahead of the gypsy moth infestation and participates in eradication of small localized gypsy moth populations. USDA-APHIS was instrumental in monitoring the gypsy moth in Michigan from the late 1950s to the early 1980s in uninfested areas. Today, APHIS deploys pheromone traps and conducts inspections in areas where introductions are likely, such as large, urban recreational areas and ports. APHIS also is responsible for developing and administering federal quarantine restrictions regulating the movement of plant material and other objects from infested to uninfested areas.

Michigan Department of Agriculture. The MDA administers Michigan's Cooperative Voluntary Gypsy Moth Suppression Program, and in general, is responsible for administering any state forest pest management project (Act 185, PA 1931). The goals of the Gypsy Moth Suppression Program are: (1) to preserve at least 60 percent of full leaf complement of treated trees, and (2) to reduce the amount of nuisance of the gypsy moth caterpillar.

As coordinator of the Michigan Gypsy Moth Suppression Program, the MDA is responsible for determining which areas might require spraying with *Bt*, when these areas should be sprayed, and how assessments of post-treatment effects will be conducted. The MDA also applies for reimbursement funds through the USDA-FS, trains aerial applicators and county personnel involved in administering *Bt*, establishes standards for pesticide applicators, and issues licenses, as outlined in Michigan Regulation No. 636.

The MDA, in cooperation with the USDA-FS, conducts an Environmental Assessment of the Michigan Gypsy Moth Suppression Project each year prior to its implementation. This Environmental Assessment is required by the National Environmental Policy Act (NEPA) for federal agencies to fund state and local pest suppression programs which might affect the human environment. The annual Environmental Assessment reports, in addition to several other Environmental Assessments conducted by the USDA-FS and the USDA-APHIS, constitute the EIS required by the Environmental Protection Agency (EPA) for any suppression project.[13]

The MDA also has financed the state-wide pheromone monitoring program that was established in 1985. Over 3,000 permanent pheromone traps are set up in a grid-like system across the state. The number of males caught in each trap and the location of these traps are stored in a database, then analyzed for changes in population and distribution from year to year. This monitoring program costs the state of Michigan about $90,000 per year. The MDA also finances a portion of the aerial defoliation survey that is conducted by the MDNR.

Finally, the MDA also provides the funds necessary to conduct the Michigan Gypsy Moth Education Program directed and administered by MSU and MSU-Extension. This program costs the state $100,000 per year and is a line item in the MDA budget.

United States Department of Agriculture-Forest Service. The Forest Service is the lead agency in the Michigan Cooperative Suppression Program, and cooperates with the MDA on cost-sharing suppression programs. The USDA-FS is provided with the authority to give technical and financial assistance to states through the Cooperative Forestry Assistance Act of 1978, as amended by the Forest Stewardship Act of 1990.[14] The USDA-FS also participates with the MDA in developing the annual Environmental Assessments and produces either an EIS if the Environmental Assessment finds potential environmental impacts for a given proposed management strategy, or it develops a FONSI statement. In Michigan, the USDA Forest Service-NASPF (Northeastern Area, State and Private Forestry), located in St. Paul, Minnesota, has played a key role in the Michigan Voluntary Cooperative Suppression Program.

The USDA-FS is responsible for managing and monitoring gypsy moths on federal lands, including National Forests, military lands, and reservations. It also has produced educational videos and pamphlets to heighten awareness about the gypsy moth problem.

Michigan Department of Natural Resources. The MDNR is responsible for monitoring defoliation through the use of sophisticated aerial videography. Costs of this program are shared between the MDA and USDA-FS. As much as 50 percent of the costs of this program are provided by the USDA-FS.

The MDNR manages public lands and decides what types of management strategies are necessary for these lands. Personnel at the MDNR analyze defoliation data to quantify the extent of the problem in the state and decide how to manage gypsy moths on state forests. This is a particularly important role for the MDNR, since Michigan has more acres of state forest land than any other state in the country. The MDNR also has the responsibility to assess impacts of potential management decisions (e.g., the application of certain chemicals) on non-target, threatened or endangered species. The MDNR's Natural Features Inventory (NFI) and the USFWS (United States Fish and Wildlife Service) determine if endangered or threatened species are located in areas to be managed for gypsy moths.

Academic Institutions. It is nearly impossible to identify all of the people at Michigan's academic institutions who have conducted research related to the gypsy moth. This is because the research conducted on such types of problems generally is broad (e.g., economic and environmental assessments to microbiology and biochemistry). The major academic institutions and their general activities include the following.

Michigan State University. There are numerous studies being conducted at MSU to aid in our understanding of how pests can affect the environment. At least eleven faculty members in the Department of Entomology are involved in some research aspect of the gypsy moth. In the Department of Entomology, for example, studies are being conducted to: (1) map the existing distribution and abundance of gypsy moths using geographic information systems, geostatistics and predictive modeling, (2) study biocontrol methods of managing the gypsy moth, (3) determine the best educational strategies to reduce the amount of public panic that normally occurs when gypsy moths first defoliate new areas, (4) study gypsy moth preference for hosts, and (5) examine the effects of insecticides and gypsy moth defoliation on non-target organisms in Michigan.

Entomologists and others work closely with MSU-Extension in all Michigan counties to distribute educational information to the public concerning the gypsy moth. Several faculty at MSU regularly contribute toward these educational documents, which are published and distributed by the Gypsy Moth Education Program.

University of Michigan. Research has been conducted on factors contributing toward tree mortality, gypsy moth host selection, and changes in species composition of the forest in gypsy moth infected areas.

PRESENT POLICY

Education. Within Michigan, there has been an effort to develop sound educational strategies so that the public can become more aware of gypsy moth biology, impacts, and management options. The Michigan Gypsy Moth Education Program (MGMEP) was established by the state legislature in 1989 and was implemented in 1990. It is the only state sponsored gypsy moth education program in the country. It receives approximately $100,000 in funds from the MDA annually. The MGMEP is directed and implemented by the Department of Entomology at Michigan State University and MSU-Extension. The MGMEP produces and distributes many educational materials including bulletins, videos, and newsletters. The MGMEP takes the lead role in teaching county level personnel the basics of gypsy moth biology and management. Representatives also provide information to the news media and are frequently invited to speak at public meetings. Recently, the MGMEP has become very active in providing materials and expertise to middle school and high school science teachers.

Support of population monitoring program to assess risk to Michigan's forests. There also has been support for large-scale monitoring of the pest distribution and abundance through a program established and implemented by the Michigan Department of Agriculture, Michigan Department of Natural Resources, and Michigan State University. The use of a permanent trapping grid has allowed biologists to monitor annual changes in the population levels of the pest at specific locations and to generate "maps" that can be used to assess the status of the population on a large scale. The maps are produced using software that employs geographic information systems (GIS). GIS allows scientists to perform complex spatial analyses on data by combining and manipulating maps. Permanent trapping grids also provide many people, such as policy analysts, with valuable information at a glance about the pest's distribution and current population status. These grids also illustrate how local populations can change rapidly over time.[15] Further, these maps aid people in predicting where the gypsy moth might move next, and how long it may take to do so. They also provide information necessary to build predictive models used by researchers and policy analysts.

The state has conducted annual aerial defoliation surveys to determine the impact of this pest on the susceptible forests. Other monitoring programs do exist, but these are more localized. In areas of high gypsy moth populations, counts of egg masses are conducted over small regions to assess the potential for defoliation. Egg mass counts generally correlate well with defoliation for that year. Thus, this method provides an excellent means to develop local management strategies and to decide if spraying is needed and at what locations. However, due to the high costs of this procedure, egg mass counts cannot be conducted over larger regions, viz., at the state level. In general, the most effective monitoring programs are the most costly, so determining which monitoring program to support requires a careful analysis of the costs and benefits of each type of program.

Control the rate of spread into unaffected areas. Recently, the USDA's Forest Service has begun a multi-state program to slow the spread of the gypsy moth into highly susceptible forest areas. Four states— Michigan, Virginia, North Carolina, and West Virginia—are involved in this project. New technologies developed in research programs will be tested to determine their value in operational projects designed to slow the rate of spread of the gypsy moth into uninfested areas. The project uses a pheromone-baited trap monitoring system, similar to the system conducted by the MDA. Pheromone traps are used to determine the location of the leading edge of large populations and to delimit special areas that may need treatment ahead of the infestation, such as urban and recreational areas. An active education and public information program has been developed to reduce risks of new gypsy moth introductions and to engender support for the project. Management decisions are made by a Technical and Steering Committee composed of project leaders from various state and federal agencies, including the MDNR, MDA, and the USDA-FS. The first year of the study in Michigan was 1993. It is anticipated that this project will continue in Michigan until 1996.

Research on alternative control agents. There has been more emphasis in recent years to move away from using insecticides in favor of using biological control agents. To date, there has been only limited success with the use of biological control agents. Agents that are used include the introduction of insect parasites, use of a fungal pathogen (*Entomophaga maimaiga*), and deployment of sterile males into the population. However, more basic research is needed to determine the potential affects of biological control agents on the environment.

KEY POLICY ISSUES

There are many lessons to be learned from our experience with controlling the gypsy moth in Michigan. The key policy questions that have been addressed and the lessons learned from attempting to solve this problem follow.

How can we evaluate the status of gypsy moth populations and potential impacts on forests, tourism, urban areas, and other sectors? Knowledge about the status of a pest population can be obtained through systematic, large-scale monitoring. An effective and informative population monitoring program requires many elements. The monitoring program must be systematic so that annual changes in population numbers are not attributable to changes in the trapping design. Further, the monitoring system also needs to be conducted in areas not known to be affected so as to adequately characterize the pest dispersal rates and how the "leading edge" of the population behaves. A sound monitoring program incorporates information about the characteristics of the environment (e.g., suitable habitat). Many monitoring systems provide data which can be analyzed using GIS. The monitoring program should also collect information about the most important aspects of the life history of the pest. As we have experienced in the gypsy moth program, the most reliable monitoring is generally the most costly; thus, there will probably be tradeoffs between the cost of monitoring and the reliability of information from any pest monitoring program.

The magnitude of the gypsy moth's impacts has been difficult to determine because they are so diverse. An economic assessment of the impact of the gypsy moth in Michigan has not been conducted except in a few sectors, such as the impact on parts of the forest products industry. However, the Michigan Gypsy Moth Suppression Program does take into account the development of policy to address the impact on sectors likely to be affected. For example, recreation areas are examined carefully for defoliation and egg masses, and these areas are treated with *Bt* when it is determined that gypsy moths will decrease their value.

Should gypsy moth population levels be controlled and what are the acceptable levels? The decision to attempt to regulate a pest's population or the damage it may cause are serious considerations. The accepted method to accomplish pest regulation is by application of a pesticide recommended by the Extension Service or another government agency responsible for the testing and evaluation of pesticides. Societal awareness of the effect of insecticides on groundwater and on the food chain has increased considerably within the last two decades. Microbial products, such as *Bacillus thuringiensis,* which are cost effective, safe, and produce acceptable levels of control, have replaced more toxic insecticides on public lands. Community-based programs have elected to use these materials due to the influence of an array of public and private interest groups which have different perspectives on the use of pesticides to manage pests like the gypsy moth. Because of these pressures and other decisions, Michigan has evolved a rational approach to gypsy moth damage suppression.

Decisions regarding pest population and pest damage suppression by homeowners and private landowners should be based on knowledge of the potential consequences of defoliation by the gypsy moth. The cyclical nature and the long duration of high populations of forest insects, tree susceptibility to damage, and tree mortality are part of the risk equation. Attitude toward the gypsy moth itself (a large, ugly, hairy caterpillar), the sheer number of the caterpillars, and the subsequent disruption caused in an area, can elicit a response of hatred toward the insect, resulting in use and often misuse of pesticides by private property owners as a means of revenge. Alternatives to chemical use tend to be more labor intensive, less effective, and take longer to impact populations. The implication of the chemicals themselves as a potential danger to human health are a component of the decision as to whether pests require regulation. The spatial extent of outbreak populations is a factor in decisionmaking because of the probability of continued expansion into previously uninfected areas. Knowledge of these interacting factors is complex and can change due to weather influences on the biology of the trees and the insect.

The philosophy of the individual has a great deal to do with the decisions of what methods to use to reduce risk to trees defoliated by the gypsy moth. The potential for tree mortality due to successive defoliations will lead most individuals to resort to population reduction strategies. In areas of high gypsy moth populations and heavy defoliation, most people will resort to pesticide application if no alternatives are available. On the other hand, some believe that pesticide use can prolong outbreaks because pesticides reduce competition and survivors tend to be reproductively robust, causing populations to rebound.

In summary, the objectives of any management program must incorporate public concerns, consequences of actions on public health and environmental health, as well as environmental and economic risks due to the pest itself. Finally, we have learned that management policy should be based on information and knowledge rather than on hearsay and panic.

What elements are necessary to develop policy to address large-scale forest pest problems? To develop prudent policy to reduce environmental and human health risks from pests, we have found that there are several key elements necessary for any management program to be successful. These are cross-agency communication and public education programs.

Communication among key groups is essential. Communication among agencies is of the utmost importance to the success of any forest management program where impacts occur over large areas. This has been especially true in this state's attempt to address the problems related to the introduction of the gypsy moth. Areas impacted include federal, state, and private forests, and thus, responsibilities for their proper management occur under different jurisdictions. In addition, any management strategies employed will likely affect other jurisdictions. In the past, key officials within the MDNR, USDA-FS, and MDA have communicated well and Michigan has benefited from this positive interaction. In some states where communication between organizations is not entirely effective, this lack of communication has contributed toward increased severity of the pest problem and a poor understanding of the pest's impact on the state's environment and economy.

A possible missing link in the current communication network is the exchange of ideas between policy analysts and researchers at universities. There have been several attempts in the past in Michigan to coordinate gypsy moth conferences. One of the most notable was the First Annual Michigan Gypsy Moth Conference held in East Lansing in 1987. Subsequent meetings have not taken place on a regular basis, leading to poor coordination of research within the state on the gypsy moth. Because risk and subsequent policies change from year to year, it is important for policy analysts and university researchers to communicate their needs on a regular basis.

Maintain a public education program. Education has been implemented in the state of Michigan to teach the public how to react to this pest and what measures are needed to reduce the impact of the gypsy moth on their property. When any policy is implemented without proper education programs in place, we have seen the public "over-react" to the gypsy moth problem.

We have learned from the gypsy moth introduction that it is important to communicate with the public and environmental organizations. For example, in 1978 the dimilin injunction against the MDA caused the MDA to completely cancel its program to control the gypsy moth that year. Also, because this organism, like most exotic pests, is dispersed by humans, a well-informed public is essential to reduce the chance of long-range dispersal. Because the gypsy moth is an urban as well as rural forest pest, its impact on the public is much greater than a pest that inhabits only remote locations. For all of these reasons, the Michigan Gypsy Moth Education Program is a necessary element in the effort to control the impact of this pest on the environment.

Education on the gypsy moth problem has focused on attempts to make the public more aware of non-chemical means of suppressing the gypsy moth in their area. Michigan State University has played a key role in developing materials for the public that are distributed through the MSU Extension Service.[16]

NOTES

1. W. V. O'Dell, "The Gypsy Moth Outbreak in Michigan," *J. Economic Entomology* 48 (1955):170-72.
2. G. A. Simmons, "History of the Gypsy Moth in Michigan," in *Gypsy Moth in Michigan: The First Annual Report of the Gypsy Moth Technical Committee,* Michigan Cooperative Forest Pest Management Annual Report, edited by B. A. Montgomery (East Lansing: Department of Entomology, Michigan State University, 1987), 87-2:8-9.

3. J. A. Whitter, J. L. Stoyenoff, and F. Sapio, "Impacts of the Gypsy Moth in Michigan," *Michigan Academician* 25 (1992):67-90.

4. M. L. McManus and T. McIntyre, "The Gypsy Moth: Research toward Integrated Pest Management," *USDA Forest Service Technical Bulletin 1584* (Washington, D.C.: Government Printing Office, 1981), 1-8.

5. United States Department of Agriculture-Animal Health Inspection Service, *Counties in the United States containing high gypsy moth populations*, 1992.

6. M. L. McManus, "The Role of Behavior in the Dispersal of Newly Hatched Gypsy Moth Larvae," USDA Forest Service Research Paper NE-267, Washington D.C., 1973.

7. S. H. Gage, T. M. Wirth, and G. A. Simmons, "Predicting Regional Gypsy Moth (Lymantriidae) Population Trends in an Expanding Population Using Pheromone Trap Catch and Spatial Analysis," *Environmental Entomology* 19 (1990):370-77; M. Hanna, "Gypsy Moth (Lepidoptera: Lymantriidae) Survey in Michigan," *Great Lakes Entomologist* 14 (1981):103-8.

8. S. H. Dreistadt, "An Assessment of Gypsy Moth Eradication Attempts in Michigan (Lepidoptera: Lymantriidae)," *Great Lakes Entomologist* 16 (1983):143-48.

9. J. A. Witter, J. L. Stoyenoff, and F. Sapio, "Impacts of the Gypsy Moth in Michigan," *Michigan Academician* 25 (1992):67-90; Hanna, "Gypsy Moth (Lepidoptera: Lymantriidae) Survey in Michigan."

10. Ibid.

11. S. H. Gage and M. E. Mispagel, "Design and Development of a Cooperative Crop Monitoring System," Conference on Automated Data Processing for Integrated Pest Management, Washington, D.C., United States Department of Agriculture, 1979.

12. Michigan Department of Agriculture, Environmental Assessment: Cooperative Gypsy Moth Suppression Project for Michigan, 1993.

13. Ibid.

14. Ibid.

15. S. H. Gage and B. C. Pijanowski, "Application of Remote Sensing and Analysis of Digital Landscape Maps to Assess Ecological Risk from Pest Populations," in *Proceedings of the 25th International Symposium on Remote Sensing and Global Environmental Change: Tools for Sustainable Development*, 4-8 April 1993, 2:390-402.

16. We would like to thank Frank Sapio of the MDNR, Ron Priest of the MDA, and Mike Connor of the USDA-FS in St. Paul, Minnesota, for providing input and answering questions during the course of this article's development. The success of the Michigan Gypsy Moth Suppression Program is due in part to their hard work and determination.

III.
Education Policy

State Education Policy and Teaching Practice: Issues Yet To Be Joined

Steve Kaagan and Diane Holt-Reynolds

PROBLEM, PURPOSE, AND STRUCTURE

In the last decade there has been an abundance of state policymaking in education, perhaps more than has occurred in the whole of this century. This is as true for Michigan as for its neighbors. The somewhat unprecedented spate of law and rule making, as well as programmatic funding, has been driven by a near frantic sense on the part of leaders across the nation that our schools are not up to par and that the state is in a more fit position than the locality to make things better. In most states, education spending is about a third of the state's total annual budget, and states cover most of the costs of education that local districts provide. While this policymaking activity has had wide ranging effects on a broad array of constituent groups, it has been curiously inattentive to one key area—the ways in which student learning and teacher development relate.

The purpose of this article is to lay bare some of the more notable effects of recent policymaking on teachers' professional roles and classroom practices and to suggest that Michigan leaders could realize more of their visions for school children by considering ways of supporting the teacher learning that is essential for effective implementation of policy. We do not raise questions here about the legitimacy or the merits of current policy directions in education; rather, we hope to point policymakers toward a set of potentially fruitful inquiries that must be made if policy in education is to become more sophisticated and purposive.

We begin with a relatively brief presentation of the alternative policy instruments that Michigan leaders have at their behest. We then recapitulate the major state policy initiatives of the last decade and cite in summary their effects on the craft of teaching. Finally, given the range of policy instruments available and the sorts of goals contemporary initiatives set, we suggest that policymakers might promote more positive outcomes for students and society if they extend the reach of policy to include teacher learning and development.

POLICYMAKING: TOOLS AND VEHICLES

Mandates. When people think of policy their minds usually turn first to lawmaking by legislative bodies. This is understandable; frequent elections featuring citizen participation and full media coverage highlight the lawmaking mechanisms of our culture. However, as important and often notorious as the policy generating function of elected lawmakers might be, it has its limitations. Lawmaking is best reserved for the "command performance" arena, the "thou shalts" needed to shape the boundaries of public endeavors. "All public school teachers shall be certified"; "All students shall be inoculated against smallpox"; and "All schools shall publish an annual report of progress" are examples of measures that mandate.

However, mandates, even when judiciously applied to areas where they may be legitimately helpful, carry certain limitations. The force of a mandate depends not only on its acceptance by those whose behavior it is meant to influence, but also on the consequences or sanctions leveled if the mandate goes unheeded. What punishment attends the failure of a child to be inoculated against smallpox? She cannot be permanently denied access to schools—a second mandate, "All children shall attend school until age 16," precludes the sanction. In reality, many education-related laws are relatively "toothless" when it comes to the negative effects of non-compliance. Consequently, viable educational policy emerges through a variety of channels and takes a variety of forms beyond lawmaking.

Binding agreements. The range of policymaking maneuvers extends beyond mandates to include, for example, agreements that school systems make with their local bargaining agents. These agreements are as binding as any set of laws. In education they may in fact be more enforceable than state statutes because they have more sets of eyes and ears watching and hearing to be sure the agreed-upon measures are implemented. In addition, there are direct consequences for violations of the agreement, through such measures as grievances, strikes and lawsuits.

Incentives. Mandates and binding agreements directly and explicitly affect human actions and interactions. These are easily recognizable forms of policy. Other types of policy vehicles exert a more subtle or perhaps indirect effect on people's actions. Most of these policy measures fall under the banner of incentives. Some are monetary; for teachers there is a monetary incentive to attain a master's degree. Others do not involve money but may be equally as powerful. There may be a strong incentive to cover certain material in class or to teach a certain way if students are publicly tested on the material and parents' and citizens' views about the quality of the school are influenced by how well students perform on the tests.

Capacity building. Mandates, binding agreements, and incentives essentially provide external motivations for people to act in ways that policymakers value. However, while motivation may be a necessary element in any decision to act, it is not always a sufficient one. Therefore, capacity building initiatives serve as policymaking tools of a different order. Suppose, for example, a state government funds a unit intended to weave together the educative functions of universities and professional associations on behalf of improved teaching or more sophisticated local governance of schools. The state would effectively, if indirectly, declare the value of the continuous learning of the professionals and citizen leaders who would benefit directly from these newly established functions.

Influential knowledge bases: Expert opinion and peer networks. Finally, policy often derives much of its shape from the thinking of those whose words will never become law, but whose ideas, timely framings, or over-simplified algorithms and recommendations find their way into professional journals and practitioners' repertoires. In education this kind of policy shaping begins most often when experts from universities or consulting firms bring the "word" to those in the field. "Outcomes education," "mastery learning," and "effective schools" became operating policy for many school districts in this way.

Increasingly, some influential approaches originate not from the heads of outside experts but from networks of local practitioners. Their ideas, algorithms, and frames have the advantage of being home-grown and are thereby often better suited to local contexts. Policies that engender the organizational capacities to serve such networks, or that provide for the hardware and software necessary for person-to-person communication, assuredly tend to undergird the policy that the networks themselves represent.

MAKING POLICY, CHANGING SCHOOLS: WHAT WE TYPICALLY DO

Taken together, the various measures described above—mandates, agreements, incentives, capacity building, and influential knowledge bases—have been widely used in Michigan and elsewhere to define what student and university graduates should give evidence of knowing. State after state—led by California and South Carolina in the mid-1980s and Kentucky in the early-1990s—has adopted more stringent high school graduation requirements, developed state-wide curriculum frameworks delineating what students should learn in math, science, and other subjects, launched more elaborate student testing programs and tightened and made more stringent the processes by which teachers gain or renew their teaching certificates.

Less typically, some forms of policy have been used to announce and instantiate a new sense of role for teachers. In selected instances such as in Rochester, New York, and Dade County, Florida, collective bargaining agreements in particular became the venue for redefining teachers' roles and responsibilities and for reshaping the place of teachers in the school decisionmaking processes.

Policymaking is unquestionably a powerful agent for fixing productive minimums and for defining a state or region's valued educational outcomes. However, we question whether this represents the extent of policymakers' legitimate fields of action. Very few states, for example, have concentrated much energy or resources in this most recent decade in building the kinds of capacities that would be needed to support their own mandates for teacher change or the stipulations that were spelled out in bargaining agreements about teachers' new roles and responsibilities. Connecticut may be one of the few that has paid some attention to this important matter. Delaware may soon become another.

We suggest that as long as policy addresses outcomes only, without simultaneously addressing the processes whereby the valued outcomes might be developed, policy as a creative agent for substantive change in schools will fail to reach its potential. Even a cursory examination points toward the serious inadequacies of product-oriented policies for achieving the important ends they intend. As policymakers, we have developed considerable expertise at codifying desired student behavior into the language of policy statements and required tests. However, defining what we want students to do, know, or understand advances the aims of education less than would be possible were we to develop equal skill coupling these definitions with concrete, policy-driven support for how teachers will develop, learn, and practice the instruction that the outcomes tacitly assume.

Student Learning Means Teacher Learning: An Imaginary Scenario. As we look at contemporary policy initiatives we must be impressed by the assiduous care policymakers typically lavish on the task of making explicit the outcomes they expect policy to achieve. With rare exceptions, however, few policy initiatives appear to take into account the teacher-initiated activities associated with prescribed outcomes. Questions about whether teachers have adequate preparation for teaching in new ways seldom surface as legitimate themes in policy deliberations.

Testing-as-incentive makes a particularly accessible example for illustrating the issue, thereby provoking a consideration of some important policy options. Imagine a new state-wide language arts test mandated for all third, fifth, and eighth graders. In creating this test, policymakers might invite classroom teachers, parents, and university experts all to collaborate in its drafting. In the process, all might agree that school children should possess a thorough, testable, working knowledge of standard English grammar and that this knowledge should become progressively sophisticated as children proceed through school. Let us suppose that this new test therefore asks children to identify instances of incorrect subject/verb agreement in the third grade; parse a sentence, i.e. label its grammatical elements, in the fifth grade; and construct an original paragraph that conforms with standard English grammar in the eighth grade.

This new test would act as an incentive for third, fifth, and eighth grade teachers to engage students in a wide range of quite different activities to ensure their readiness to perform well on this test. Third graders would spend time practicing how to judge the agreement between subjects and verbs in sentences composed by someone else. Eighth graders, for their part, would spend time practicing actual composition.

None of this appears at first glance to implicate teachers' instructional repertoires in any meaningful way. However, look more closely. Consider what a teacher would need to do to generate, arrange, supervise, and help students in order to provide the instruction this imaginary test tacitly assumes. Third grade teachers would need to develop materials to illustrate correct and incorrect instances of subject/verb agreement—lots of them. Student practice leads inevitably to teacher generation of materials with which to do the practicing. Even if the imaginary school board of this imaginary school were far-sighted enough to allocate funds for the purchase of published practice materials, teachers would still need to edit these for the progress levels of the individual students in classrooms, arrange class time to include multiple, repeated opportunities to practice with the materials, develop a repertoire for explaining what makes some sentences correct while others are less acceptable, rearrange countless pieces of the existing language arts curriculum, and integrate these changes with the rest of the third grade curricular day.

Meanwhile, the eighth grade teachers who see students for only fifty minutes each day would need to adjust curriculum plans and demands to make time for students to write regularly, attend to teacher-led feedback about that writing, revise and then confer with the teacher about the adequacy of revisions. These adjustments depend, of course, on the teachers' ability to read the writing of as many as thirty students in each of five or six separate classes often enough to make the practice worthwhile. These teachers would also need extensive expertise in noting, redirecting, and monitoring students' progress in revising a range of very broad writing objectives.

On top of all else the tests would require that teachers develop these instructional practices in classrooms while children are present and impressing immediate needs on their teachers. The new tests would certainly serve as powerful catalysts for change, but tests alone would provide teachers with no direction or help in adapting current teaching practices or developing new ones in the service of the tests.

It is highly unlikely that the imaginary policymakers would also see to it that teachers have opportunities to learn how to teach to this test. We have no data-driven hypotheses about why this would be so unlikely. Scanning current policy, including mandates, binding agreements, incentives, or expert advice only highlights the absence of this sort of attention — it does little to tell us what makes the inattention an understandable phenomenon.

Perhaps the policymakers in this imaginary scenario are not aware of the relationship between how children represent learning on a test and how they would need to practice as they prepare for that test. Perhaps they have not paused to notice that each test asks students to demonstrate their learning in a different way, that each of those ways requires a different set of preparatory instructional moves on the part of classroom teachers, and that those differing types of instructional activities emanate from very different beliefs about what it means to "learn to write" well—for example, not every teacher would be convinced that recognizing correct sentence construction in third grade leads to independent production of sentence structures in eighth grade.

Perhaps these imaginary policymakers pay so little attention to teacher learning because they assume that teachers already know how to teach in ways that foster more complete learning. Or maybe they think that teacher certification implies expansive teaching virtuosity and that teachers only need to be prompted by policymakers to produce specific instructional practices from a previously mastered range. Perhaps they assume that teachers know how to craft, guide, and integrate materials consistent with the new test; they have adequate expertise in debriefing students after using the materials; and they are well prepared to teach in ways that maximize their students' opportunities to learn to represent their knowledge in the ways the test demands—they just cannot put all these things together and carry out what is needed.

The scenario may be imaginary, but the issue is quite real. When policy defines a desired student behavior, it inherently projects into classrooms a set of teacher moves that are intended to foster, sustain, and nurture that behavior. In fact, all policy aimed directly at students aims indirectly at teachers. We might like to think that, while defining student outcomes is within our province as policymakers, we avoid policy that infringes on the proper professional domain of teachers. "How they teach should be within their professional discretion," we argue.

It is time to face the impossibility of this stance. Policy that defines student outcomes tacitly predicts teaching practice. Rather than worry about whether this impinges on teachers' discretion or status, we might do well to honor their work as professionals by supporting their opportunities to learn new, better, or simply different instructional moves. We might craft policies to support their learning and their development of ever-broader repertoires.

Comparisons with Other Areas of Endeavor. This silence, this inattention to how teachers will learn practices that are likely to bring about desired outcomes or how universities and other organizations will develop programs that produce teachers with required characteristics, contrasts with a virtual roar of activity in other settings. In most areas of endeavor, questions abound regarding the effects of a particular measure on the line worker—the person who, when all outside influences leave off, we must rely on to get the job done. In industry, this on-the-line policy enactor might be the machine operator, field representative, or service agent. In education, it is, without contradiction, the classroom teacher.

Political correctness aside, comparing teachers to line workers is worth pursuing for a moment. In industry the person who implements a policy regarding quality of manufacturing is a technician whose work-related actions are highly circumscribed. This technician works with inert materials, the properties and interactional parameters of which are well-known and predictable. Yet, policymakers in industry assume that new quotas, standards or designs will require that the technicians receive additional training, new equipment, and perhaps some temporary relief from quotas while they learn to operate the new machines and perform the new routines. A mistake stemming from lack of adequate training may result in production delays or personal injury. The risk is not worth taking.

Teachers—those who enact educational policy in this industrial model equivalent—work in dynamic interaction with "materials" that have minds, wills, and agendas of their own. The properties of these human "materials" are almost uncharted, wildly unpredictable, and various, and the consequences of a teacher's mistake will ripple through the intellectual life of the child and the classroom in equally unpredictable ways. Is this kind of risk worth taking?

As educational policymakers with an eye to reform we operate as if we know very little about what teachers who work with living, thinking, culturally immersed, diverse, and imaginative young people must do to effect a change in how they interact with these human materials in classrooms. Policy initiatives in education do not typically offer even bare minimum, industry-like levels of support for the changes in teaching practices on which student outcomes are based. We believe that Michigan leaders can seize options that will allow us to act with greater vision. An explicit, frank examination of the sets of assumptions about teachers, their practices and their learning that seem to drive product-centered policies appears to be a fruitful place to begin.

NEEDED: POLICY OPTIONS TO SUPPORT MORE EFFECTIVE TEACHING

Summary. If Michigan leaders want to move toward a better educational system in the next century they will have to shape for themselves and their constituents a much more balanced policy portfolio, one that takes into account the needs of the line worker in education, the teacher.

Such a portfolio will include mandates, but only when directives are manifestly necessary and when these directives can be accompanied by effective sanctions. It will rely on the collective bargaining process to work in those arenas where it has the greatest potential to do so. Matters of working conditions, terms of employment and now especially, the role of various interested parties in school decisionmaking processes are some of these arenas. It will provide incentives in a way that capitalizes on teachers' professional knowledge and spirit of inquiry. In no case should the results of accepting or adapting to an incentive inhibit teachers' initiative and risk taking on behalf of children's learning.

This policy portfolio will also include a conscious strategy for capacity building, providing especially for teachers' learning both as individuals and collectively and for organized support of teacher development through both new and existing institutions, either by themselves or in consortial arrangements. Finally, it will seek to affect the market for expert opinion by ensuring that teachers themselves have greater access to each other as resources in non-didactic situations, rather than consistently being placed in the position of passive listeners at the feet of outside experts.

In fact the latter two—capacity building and expert opinion—are presently the two most undersupported yet potentially fertile areas for policy formulation in the decade ahead. If, for example, the state would take the lead in leveraging institutional capacity on behalf of teacher learning and development and would simultaneously provide base support for the convening of affiliational groups of teachers interested in professional growth, the result would likely be increased cooperation between policymakers and policy enactors. The beneficiaries of such cooperation would be the children, youth, and families of the state.

In sum, we believe that the policy strides of this last decade leave considerable room for improvement. As we take seriously the role of the teacher as the implementor of policy, as we treat teachers as professionals with a disposition to learn, develop and practice an expanding repertoire of skills, questions and visions, so will we craft policy in ways that support learning for all—both students and their teachers.

REFERENCES

Cohen, D. K., M. W. McLaughlin, and J. E. Talbert. (1993). *Teaching for Understanding: Challenges for Policy and Practice.* San Francisco: Jossey-Bass.

Elmore, R. F., and McLaughlin. (1988). *Steady Work: Policy, Practice, and the Reform of American Education.* National Institute of Education Series #R-3574-NIE/RC. Santa Monica, California: Rand Corporation.

Elmore, R. F. (1990). *Restructuring Schools: The Next Generation of Educational Reform.* San Francisco: Jossey-Bass.

Firestone, W. A., B. D. Bader, D. Massel, and S. Rosenblum. (1992). "Recent Trends in State Educational Reform: Assessment and Prospects." *Teachers College Record* 94(2):254-78.

Fuhrman, S. H. (1993). *Designing Coherent Education Policy: Improving the System.* San Francisco: Jossey-Bass.

Kerchner, C. T., and J. E. Koppich. (1993). *A Union of Professionals: Labor Relations and Education Reform.* New York: Teachers College Press.

McCarthy, M. (1990). "Teacher Testing Programs." In *The Educational Reform Movement of the 1980s,* Joseph Murphy, ed. Berkeley: McCutchan Publishing.

Odden, A. R. (1991). *Education Policy Implementation.* Albany: SUNY Press.

The Transition from School to Work

Phyllis T. H. Grummon

THE CHANGING WORLD OF WORK

Sometime in the last twenty years or so, the rules about how young adults move from school to work changed. In the past, high school graduates, and even those without a diploma, could expect to find employment relatively easily and to earn enough money to maintain a middle class existence. While this was most true immediately following World War II, the ability of youth to find well-paying work changed little until the late 1960s and early 1970s. What has happened since the early 1970s is that real earnings for high school graduates have fallen by an average of 28 percent.[1] A pattern emerges of youth between the ages of sixteen and twenty-five finding employment primarily in low-paying ($4-6 an hour) jobs in what is called the secondary labor market.[2] While a young person may be employed full-time following high school in such a job, it is virtually impossible to save money, start a family, or even move away from home. The shift from manufacturing to service sector jobs has meant that even those with a high school diploma are unlikely to find well-paying work.

In addition to the loss of manufacturing jobs, those jobs that do pay middle class wages have changed too. By-and-large, far more skills, both academic and interpersonal, are needed to enter and advance in jobs. The ability to work with a variety of technologies, to use statistics and mathematics to analyze problems, to read and interpret complex manuals, and to work in teams are now routinely required in all sectors of the economy. Any number of surveys of employers, both formal and informal, reveal they are seeking employees with an ability to learn even more than those with any specific skills.[3] So, students leaving high school are likely to find that what they learned will be insufficient to allow them to enter more than a minimum wage job, the same job they had while in high school. Given that the majority of students either do not go on to postsecondary education or do not complete that education, the need for K-12 schools to respond is critical.

Michigan represents a somewhat different picture than the rest of the nation because it still has a relatively strong manufacturing base. The effects of the change in manufacturing jobs, both their decline in numbers and the increase in skills needed to perform in those jobs, were felt in Michigan earlier than in most parts of the country. These effects prompted Michigan's manufacturers, primarily auto companies and their suppliers, to take steps to increase training in their workforces and their involvement in educational policy. In addition, before the end of the decade, manufacturers in Michigan will be faced with significant numbers of retirements in the skilled trades. These retirements mean that manufacturers must now find ways to begin training replacements.

KEY POLICY QUESTIONS

The issuance of "A Nation At Risk" in 1983 sparked broad concern in the country about the quality of K-12 education. Its focus was the need to get "back to basics." There was a general sense that if enough money was available, schools would be able to teach students what they needed to know, and what they needed to know better were the "3 Rs." Much of the focus was on increasing teacher salaries and using more traditional instructional methods, such as rote memorization and testing. Schools and educational policy in the 1980s generally followed the path set out in "A Nation At Risk."

By the late 1980s, business became more involved in schools and educational reform. From a business perspective, the "3 Rs" were not enough. Business came to the forefront of the education reform debate by clearly stating its need for the "up-skilling" of the future labor force in more than just reading, writing, and arithmetic. Government, at all levels, responded to that push from business. A number of commissions were formed and studies were published, the most notable of which was the Secretary's Commission on Achieving Necessary Skills (SCANS). The focus of these efforts was to describe the range of skills that the most progressive, "high performance" workplaces needed. SCANS, in particular, not only described those skills, but also pushed for the development of ways to assess students and adults on those skills. SCANS suggested that if assessments existed, they would act as a prod to schools and job training programs to ensure that students had the skills needed for success in better paying, more highly-skilled jobs.

Education has shown a mixed reaction to the push from business and the government to direct more of their efforts to preparing students for work. Some educational groups have become concerned that redesigning the curriculum for workforce preparation may result in tracking students in such a way that they will not be able to go on to college if they want. Other educators question the emphasis put on workforce preparation. They worry that the general good of having an educated citizenry will be lost in the drive to make sure everyone can have a job after high school. Finally, some educators question the wisdom of the involvement of businesses in education when, in many instances, they do not train their own workers. They suggest that businesses need to make sure they are functioning as high performance organizations that can use highly-skilled workers before blaming problems on schools.

The concerns of businesses, the government, and education have been played out in the policy arenas of curriculum reform and school restructuring. While education has expressed reservations about making workforce preparation the sole focus of curriculum change, it has been included as part of that change in most states and districts. What we find, then, is that concern about the ability of students to make the transition from school to work is part of a number of larger education and policy agendas. Federal, state, and local entities involved in education, employment, and training have all addressed this transition. The key policy questions with which they have grappled are:

- What instruction is needed in order to successfully prepare students for the workplace?
- How should that instruction be delivered?
- How do we build a coherent system for helping students make the transition to work?

These are questions that involve not only how policy can help or hinder schools in these efforts, but also the very nature of the educational experience—how teachers teach, how students learn and how schools are structured to facilitate teaching and learning.

While the goal of this article is not to discuss school reform and restructuring in great depth, it is necessary to describe some of the changes that seem to be required if the policies and programs trying to facilitate the school-to-work transition are to be successful. Most discussions of school reform focus on the reality that our present system for delivering instruction has not changed significantly since the advent of the industrial revolution. Whether explicitly or not, our schools function like the assembly lines of the past, where students (and workers) were required to keep their attention only on the work in front of them, were given the same work to do over and over, and where the ability to follow directions was the most highly valued social interaction. As described briefly above, the most competitive, high-wage workplaces of today and the future no longer require these skills. These workplaces require workers who can think critically, solve problems, work in teams, and make decisions based on information they have collected. In the past, these functions were reserved for management. Thus, if schools are to meet the needs of the labor market for more highly-skilled workers and the needs of their students for more meaningful careers, they need to deliver education in a way more like the way work is done now, and not the way it was done in the past.

School reform efforts are also based on research in learning and cognition. Such research indicates that students are more likely to be successful when they are actively engaged in the discovery and construction of knowledge.[4] Instruction is frequently problem focused, rather than subject matter focused, so that students learn the content and skills they need to solve a problem and not just content in isolation from its application. These newer pedagogies also emphasize the ability of every student to learn, while recognizing that students vary in their preferred learning styles.

It has been difficult in many cases, however, to translate this research into classroom practice. Teachers have not traditionally been trained to act as coaches and facilitators of learning, but rather they have been trained to dispense knowledge. Schools are not physically structured to encourage movement by students among various learning activities and with each other. Parents can also be resistant to these new kinds of instruction. A classroom where students are loud, potentially all working on different projects, and not learning by rote looks very different from what parents experienced in school and consider "good" education. Finally, our means of judging school effectiveness are based on content knowledge and seat time, not on the acquisition of skills related to measurable and desired outcomes.

Thus, it is likely that the ability of programs focused on the transition from school-to-work to meet success will be affected by the presence or absence of school reform efforts. In some cases, school-to-work concerns may drive the school reform process. In other cases, such programs may not be able to be instituted because of the lack of broader school restructuring. Regardless of the state or stage of school reform efforts, there are a number of programs, both new and ongoing, designed to help students in the transition to work. Those efforts will be discussed in the next section of this article.

PAST AND PRESENT SCHOOL-TO-WORK INITIATIVES

Many schools have been involved in some form of workforce preparation for a number of years. Often these are relatively low-key efforts to help students learn about different careers. Career education has existed in secondary schools for a number of decades. Classes in career education may help students learn about what education and training are required for different careers and how their personal styles or preferences relate to career choices. Job shadowing, the opportunity to follow someone on a job for a day or more, may be associated with career education classes. Some students work in cooperative education programs where they work in a local business and attend school, usually taking business or general education courses. The opportunity to participate in one or more of these efforts varies greatly by school and even by the teachers involved. This diminishes their usefulness as school-to-work programs.

The preparation of youth for the workforce has been among the issues at the top of the agenda for the past two federal administrations. One of the first initiatives to be put forward in relationship to this issue was the 1990 amendments to the Carl D. Perkins Act. This act, which was instrumental in promoting vocational education in the 1980s, was substantially revised in 1990 to focus on the issues of school and systemic reform and the integration of academic and vocational instruction. Under the 1990 Perkins Act, funds were targeted at the integration of skills-based curricula between secondary and postsecondary institutions. The Perkins Act also required, because of its funding formulas, that local districts and educational entities join together in consortia to help ensure that programs were of sufficient size and scope to be effective and to enable access for targeted groups (e.g., economically or academically disadvantaged youth, disabled youth, students with limited English proficiency, etc.).[5] The Tech Prep Education Act included in the Perkins re-authorization focused on the need to reframe vocational and technical education.[6] As conceived in this legislation, Tech Prep is designed to provide students with more applied education in secondary and postsecondary schools and to specify the skills that students should acquire in each setting. These skills should prepare students for a scientific, technical, health, agriculture, or business career through a course of study in a Tech Prep program.

The first three years of grants to local consortia were designed to help them plan for systemic change, provide in-service training for faculty, create partnerships with businesses, and design careers-based skill sequences between secondary and postsecondary programs. This has meant that only now are some Tech Prep programs beginning to realize the goals of the program. In most places, with Michigan being no exception, Tech Prep as a means for helping youth transition to work exists more on paper than in classrooms or schools.

Just as vocational education is being transformed into Tech Prep, traditional apprenticeship programs are also being reconsidered. For many years, a small but consistent number of students were served by entering apprenticeships for construction and the skilled trades.[7] As policymakers became concerned with the transition from school to work and with our global competitiveness, they looked to the ways in which other countries use apprenticeships.[8] It was clear that many countries, Germany being the most advanced example, used work-based learning and apprenticeships to prepare the majority of youth for entry into the adult labor market. These findings have led to an effort to expand youth apprenticeships in this country, both for non-traditional students (e.g., women and minorities into traditional apprenticeships) and into non-traditional areas (e.g., beyond construction and skilled trades). The U.S. Department of Labor has funded a number of projects, including fifteen in Michigan, to help develop more youth apprenticeship opportunities.

While focused on those presently employed, the development of industry skills standards is another federal initiative that has clear implications for transitions in the labor force. Twenty-five national industry groups are working under the auspices of the U.S. Departments of Labor and Education on the development of skills standards for a variety of occupations, from health to banking to metal working. These skills standards would form the basis for identifying portable skills: skills designed to enable workers to move between jobs in the same industry and across industries. Clearly, if such standards can be developed and agreed on by an industry, they should have a significant influence on curriculum, instruction, and assessment whether for secondary students or those already in the workforce. This could be particularly true for those skills that appear in more than one set of industry standards.

All of these efforts are subsumed, to some degree, under proposed federal legislation to develop school-to-work opportunities systems in states.[9] In anticipation of the passage of that legislation, the Departments of Labor and Education are presently using existing funds to promote state level planning and implementation of school-to-work programs. The stated purposes of the legislation are to:

> (1) establish a national framework within which all States can create statewide School-to-Work Opportunities systems that are integrated with the systems developed under the Goals 2000: Educate America Act and that offer young Americans access to a performance-based education and training program that will enable them to earn portable credentials, prepare them for a first job in a high-skill, high-wage career, and increase their opportunities for further education;
> (2) transform workplaces into active learning components by making employers full partners in providing high-quality, work-based learning experiences to students.[10]

The program would allow states to build on present initiatives, such as Tech Prep and youth apprenticeships. However, they must demonstrate how local programs will be disseminated and how they will build a state-wide, systemic change effort to promote the purpose of the legislation. In addition, the legislation requires that programs have the following common features and basic program components:

(a) The basis of the School-to-Work Opportunities system is: (1) The integration of work-based learning and school-based learning; (2) The integration of occupational and academic learning; and (3) The linking of secondary and postsecondary education.

(b) School-to-Work Opportunities programs will result in students attaining: (1) A high school diploma; (2) A certificate or diploma recognizing successful completion of one or two years of postsecondary education, if appropriate; and (3) A skill certificate.[11]

Both existing and proposed laws are designed to help states unify their efforts into state-wide systems for enabling youth to move into the labor force more effectively. While not overly prescriptive, the School-to-Work Opportunities system provides some answers to the policy questions posed above. It suggests that students need instruction at work sites as well as in the classroom. It supports a strong counseling program, both for career exploration and for the maintenance of high academic standards. Finally, it suggests strategies for working with employers to build links that enable students to participate in work-based learning, as well as to move students into the labor force.

MICHIGAN'S SCHOOL-TO-WORK INITIATIVES

In 1988 Michigan was among the first states to gather information from employers on their needs for workplace skills.[12] Through a state-wide task force and a survey of employers, three basic areas of need were identified: academic, personal management, and teamwork skills. This information was used to help frame the outcomes for employability skills in the state's model core curriculum associated with Public Act 25 of 1990. They also served as the basis for the development of an employability skills assessment. This assessment is designed to be developmental and uses a portfolio to help students learn what skills are needed and the level of skills they presently possess.[13] Both of these initiatives represent efforts aimed at all students in Michigan, regardless of their post-high school plans.

As discussed briefly above, Michigan also has fifteen pilot youth apprenticeship and thirty-nine Tech Prep consortia operating throughout the state. The largest youth apprenticeship pilot involves approximately 50-100 high school students in the Flint area. The other apprenticeship programs are all smaller and none of the programs has been in existence long enough to graduate any students into either community college programs or formal apprenticeships. Virtually every school district in the state is participating in at least one Tech Prep consortium. Each consortium consists of one or more high schools, an intermediate school district, and a community college. School districts may elect to be in one or more consortia. As with most education in Michigan, there is a high degree of local control over the ways in which consortia have gone about planning for Tech Prep implementation. The 1993-94 academic year represents the first year in which consortia will be moving from planning to formal implementation. Needless to say, a number of consortia have already begun programming with students that they consider to be part of their Tech Prep initiative.

Two other initiatives have some relevance to policy discussions in Michigan.[14] In August of 1992, a Blue Ribbon Commission on Career/Technical Education presented its report to then Speaker of the House, Lewis Dodak.[15] This report outlined a number of recommendations related to the transition from school to work, as well as the ongoing training and development of presently employed workers. While none of the specific recommendations has been put forward as legislation in Michigan, many recommendations mirror those seen in the federal legislation and the School-to-Work Opportunities proposal. Thus, the thinking done by this Commission may still find its way into Michigan policy and practice through federal legislation.

The second initiative of relevance to school-to-work was the creation by executive order of the Michigan Jobs Commission in 1993. The Commission has been constructed to encourage the coordination among virtually all of the state's efforts associated with workforce development and participation, as well as business attraction and development. Over time, any program which has any of these goals as its purpose has been brought into the Commission so it now includes programs and employees from the Departments of Education, Commerce, Social Services, Labor, Natural Resources and the Michigan Employment Security Commission. The Jobs Commission is composed of 140 people and 1/3 of a billion dollars worth of program responsibilities.[16] The workforce development side of the Commission, the Michigan Jobs Team, focuses primarily on programs and funds associated with the training and re-training of laid-off or presently employed workers. However, it is also involved in the youth apprenticeship programs and will be coordinating the state's response to the School-to-Work Opportunities initiative. The extent to which school-to-work initiatives are realized in Michigan is likely to be influenced by the role the Commission plays in the overall development of Michigan's workforce. If the Jobs Commission views it as a high priority, then it is likely to move forward either on its own, or in conjunction with broader school reform efforts.

In summary, Michigan and the nation have developed a number of strategies to begin to help students' transitions into work in a more coherent fashion. These efforts represent a range of intervention levels. At one level, job shadowing and cooperative work placements are used in some high schools to help students learn about work and career options. The Employability Skills Portfolio represents a way in which all students in the state have the opportunity to learn what generic skills are desired in the workplace, as well as what skills they have developed. Career planning curricula are also broadly available to students in the state. At a more intensive level, Tech Prep, youth apprenticeship programs, vocational education, and the newer School-to-Work Opportunities system represent comprehensive programs for educating, training, and placing youth into jobs. While a variety of initiatives exist in Michigan, as they do nationally, the answers to the policy questions posed in the section above require a closer look at some of the issues associated with the how and what of learning and the how of a coherent system for moving from school to work.

POLICY OPTIONS

As Michigan or any state seeks to build a coherent system for enabling smooth transitions into the labor force, there are a number of key challenges that must be overcome. The first of these challenges is how to encourage business participation in the training and development of youth. Even Germany with its longstanding system routinely faces a lack of work sites for apprenticeships.[17] While a number of strategies for involving students in work-based learning require less commitment from businesses than apprenticeships, to be successful any system must find a way to bring students into contact with work in a more formal way than just after-school jobs. The costs to businesses of supplying work site mentors, on-the-job training, and coordinated links to schools cannot be overlooked. At this point, businesses that have been involved with pilots in youth apprenticeship or Tech Prep have had some of those costs offset by grant funds. In the long run, however, it is likely that some form of incentives or penalties will be necessary for businesses to stay involved in the training and development of youth.

If businesses become more involved in the education and training of youth, they are also likely to want a more direct say in determining what and how instruction is delivered. Again, turning to Germany as a model, we find that business works closely with education to guide the content and process of instruction. Students spend part of their time learning both academic material and workplace skills at work sites. Their time in classrooms is directed at learning applied academics and the broad skills and information needed in the occupational area they are entering. In this country there traditionally has been little interaction between business and education on the specifics of education, particularly general education. If coherent school-to-work systems are to be developed, then both parties need to find ways to communicate. Businesses must feel confident that students are receiving the instruction they need to develop workplace skills. Educators must feel comfortable they are meeting both broad educational goals and the more targeted needs identified by businesses. Since there is no history of such dialogue, school-to-work systems must develop opportunities for this to take place.

While the federal initiatives suggest that such dialogue needs to occur, we do not have any identified cases where it has developed over time and is now part of the fabric of a community. Indeed, because of the size of our labor market and the mobility of workers, local and even state partnerships may be of limited utility. If national skills standards can be developed, then they may form the basis for local agreements between businesses and schools about the skills students need to acquire, while maintaining students' abilities to look beyond the local labor market for employment. Given that only twenty-five industries are participating in the development of skills standards now (Germany has 380 identified occupational categories[18]), it is clear that much remains to be done to facilitate discussions between education and business on skill development. Until such discussions occur and consensus is reached, general education is likely to be hesitant to develop skill-based instruction for business, and business will be reluctant to assume that a student graduating from high school has certifiable skills.

If, as it appears, it will take many years to build national agreements on the skill requirements of specific occupations, what can local and state entities do in the meantime to promote the school-to-work transition? A number of states have answered this question by focusing on career development and exploration for all students. Michigan students are no exception as they are required to include evidence of career exploration in their school portfolios.[19] States reported to have the most advanced methods for promoting the school-to-work transition also have focused on the inclusion of more applied academics in their general education curricula.[20] Of concern to policymakers has been assuring that applied academic courses are accepted at postsecondary institutions as evidence for admission. States that are moving to outcomes-based education and performance-based graduation requirements are also working closely with their institutions of higher education to ensure that the demonstration of skills through certificates of mastery is acceptable for admission to 2- and 4-year colleges.

While certainly not the only other issue that must be addressed, the final issue to be discussed here is one covered more extensively in another article in this volume (see Kaagan and Holt-Reynolds)—the need for professional development for secondary school personnel. Most educators have little experience with any work setting other than education. At a minimum this reduces their ability to provide students with meaningful examples of how academic principles apply in work settings. It also affects their ability to offer career development and counseling to students. Programs that bring teachers into industry settings have proven very successful in helping teachers in these areas, but they have only been available to a very limited number of people.

Professional development is also needed to help teachers learn how to teach the more applied academic courses. The instructional strategies required for these courses are different from those used for college preparatory classes, although many strategies may be useful for both types of students. Applied courses tend to use more problem-focused, versus content-focused, learning strategies. Often, too, applied academic courses try to teach explicitly such generic skills as critical thinking and problem solving. This also affects the instructional content and strategies. Since most teachers were trained to deliver content-focused courses, there is clearly a need to provide them with training in how to deliver academic concepts in more applied and problem-focused ways.

CONCLUSION

The need to assist most students in the transition from school to work has been growing for a number of years. However, it is only in the last few years that policymakers have turned their attention to finding ways to promote this transition more systematically. A number of federal initiatives have been put forth to encourage states to develop school-to-work transition programs. These programs require that students have the opportunity to participate in work-based learning while still in high school. This may take a variety of forms from youth apprenticeships to job shadowing. School-to-work initiatives also emphasize a change in instruction to make it more applied in its focus. Finally, these initiatives promote the development of ongoing discussion between business and education. The goal of this dialogue is to help youth develop the skills actually desired by businesses and to facilitate their placement in meaningful employment following graduation.

The development of coherent systems for helping students move from school to work will take many years. Among the challenges that must be faced is the need to help businesses offset the costs for bringing students into the workplace for education and training. Money must also be spent on professional development for secondary school staffs if they are to change how and what instruction is delivered, as well as to expand their ability to provide useful and timely career guidance. Professional development can occur at a local or even an individual classroom level. However, incentives or other methods for encouraging businesses to work with education and students will need to be addressed at least at a state, if not national, level.

Finally, we must recognize that while most students are likely to find work initially in their local communities, in the long run, if we are training them for high-wage, high-skill careers, they need to have career mobility at the national level. This makes it critical for national skills standards to be developed. These standards need to be recognized as truly portable. They also must be written in a way that is useful to school personnel in the development of curriculum and instruction.

The move to develop a coherent and effective system for educating and training youth for the workplace is long overdue. In order to be realized, however, it will take coordinated effort at the local, state, and national levels. The last few years have seen the beginning of such coordination, but there is much more to be done. In the last analysis, our ability to remain competitive economically may rely on how quickly and how well we can create orderly transitions from school to work for students.

NOTES

1. Education Writers Association, *First Jobs: Young Workers in a Changing Economy* (Washington, D.C.: Education Writers Association, 1990), 3; Policy Information Center, *From School to Work* (Princeton, New Jersey: Educational Testing Service, 1990), 5.
2. S. Hamilton, *Apprenticeship for Adulthood: Preparing Youth for the Future* (New York: The Free Press, 1990), 3.
3. A. Carnevale, L. Gainer, and A. Meltzer, *Workplace Basics: The Essential Skills Employers Want* (San Francisco: Jossey-Bass, 1990); W. Mehrens, *Michigan Employability Skills Technical Report* (East Lansing: Michigan State University [William Mehrens], 1989).
4. P. Grummon, "Learning: The Balance between the Immutable and the Chaotic" (Iowa City: American College Testing, Center for Education and Work, 1993); L. Resnick, *Education and Learning to Think* (Washington, D.C.: National Academy Press, 1987).
5. General Accounting Office, *Vocational Education: Status in School Year 1990-91 and Early Signs of Change at Secondary Level*, GAO/HRD-93-71 (Washington, D.C: U.S. General Accounting Office, 1993), 3-4.
6. C. Dornsife, *Beyond Articulation: The Development of Tech Prep Programs* (Macomb, Illinois: National Center for Research in Vocational Education, 1992), 10-14.
7. Employment and Training Administration, *Work-Based Learning: Training America's Workers* (Washington, D.C.: U.S. Department of Labor, 1989), 7.
8. General Accounting Office, *Training Strategies: Preparing Noncollege Youth for Employment in the U. S. and Foreign Countries*, GAO/HRD-90-88 (Washington, D.C.: U.S. General Accounting Office 1990), 33-40.
9. *Federal Register* 58, no. 197 (Thursday, 14 October 1993): 53388-92.
10. HR 2884, S 1361, School-to Work Opportunities Act, pending federal legislation.
11. *Federal Register* 58, no. 197 (Thursday, 14 October 1993): 53388-92; HR 2884, S 1361, School-to Work Opportunities Act, pending federal legislation.
12. Governor's Task Force on Employability Skills. "Report to the Governor's Commission on Jobs and Economic Development: A Michigan Employability Profile" (Lansing, Michigan: Governor's Commission on Jobs and Economic Development, April, 1988), 3-5; W. Mehrens, *Michigan Employability Skills Technical Report* (East Lansing: Michigan State University [William Mehrens]), 1989).
13. P. Grummon, "Assessing Educational Outcomes: Trends and Opportunities" in *Policy Choices: Framing the Debate for Michigan's Future*, vol. 1, edited by T.

Bynum, J. Cutcher-Gershenfeld, P. Grummon, B. Mullan, K. Roberts, and C. Weissert (East Lansing: Michigan State University Press, 1993), 151-66.

14. Clearly, the passage of SB 1 which eliminated property tax as a means of operating schools is likely to have a significant effect on any reform efforts associated with school-to-work programming. However, when this article was written, there was yet no resolution as to how school funding would be structured or what other educational reforms might be tied to finance changes.

15. Speaker's Blue Ribbon Commission on Career/Technical Education, *Redefining the Purpose of Education: Providing Students with a Seamless Transition from School to Work* (Lansing: Michigan House of Representatives, August 1992).

16. Michigan Jobs Commission, *Partners* (Lansing: Michigan Jobs Commission, September/October, 1993), 1.

17. S. Hamilton, *Apprenticeship for Adulthood: Preparing Youth for the Future* (New York: The Free Press, 1990), 33; *Education Week* 13, no. 3 (22 September 1993):15.

18. General Accounting Office, *Training Strategies: Preparing Noncollege Youth for Employment in the U. S. and Foreign Countries,* GAO/HRD-90-88 (Washington, D.C,: U.S. General Accounting Office, 1990), 36.

19. P. Grummon, "Assessing Educational Outcomes."

20. General Accounting Office, *Transition From School to Work: States Are Developing New Strategies to Prepare Students for Jobs,* GAO/HRD-93-139 (Washington, D.C.: U.S. General Accounting Office, 1993), 18-53.

IV.
Urban Policy

Services for High Risk Youth in Detroit/Wayne County: Overview, Impact, and Implications

Marilyn L. Flynn

INTRODUCTION

The problems of youth in Detroit are of interest for several reasons. Issues of segregation, poverty, drug trafficking, unemployment, school deterioration, out-migration of the middle class, "white flight," health and social service needs, tax base erosion, and poor public image have plagued the city with increasing ferocity for the past three decades. The impacts of racism and income inequality have been especially troublesome for Detroit, because the city has less diversity and higher concentrations of African-American residents than any other major urban municipality in the United States.

If Detroit can succeed at urban redevelopment, the city will have challenged the same devils which threaten other urban communities in this state and elsewhere—and will have won against even greater economic and social odds. Implications of Detroit's struggles may be especially meaningful for the fifteen other cities in the United States with closely comparable population size, racial diversity and city/county governmental relations.[1] Within Michigan, the success of

189

Detroit's worst-off neighborhoods—or their social and economic collapse—bears important messages for all urban areas with pockets of concentrated poverty and racial or ethnic segregation.

It is accepted conventional wisdom that the youth in economically declining communities represent one vital cornerstone upon which future hopes for revitalization can rest. However, in the case of Wayne County children and youth there are many disturbing signs of academic, social, or emotional failure. In fact a 1989 survey by The Children and Youth Initiative of Detroit/Wayne County found that approximately 250,000 children and youth under seventeen received one or more services in programs for at-risk youth during a 2-week sample period.[2] This represented 38 percent of all children in the county.

Perhaps the single most dramatic indicator of stress and deprivation among the city's youth was the public assistance rate among those age seventeen or under. It is important to recall that public assistance payments in Michigan, as in other states, maintain families at below-subsistence levels. This means that benefits are not sufficient to meet minimum daily needs for clothing, shelter, food, and other necessities.

During a sample one-month period in 1989, The Children and Youth Initiative of Detroit/Wayne County estimated that 172,455 Wayne County children and youth, ages 0-18, were receiving one or more forms of public assistance. Of this number, 28,972 were adolescents, 14-17 years old, representing approximately 35 percent of all youth in this age group living in the city. The overwhelming majority were African American (95.3 percent).[3]

The geographic distribution of children and youth receiving assistance benefits was pervasive throughout the city, but family poverty was especially prevalent in some readily identifiable neighborhoods. The concentration of poverty and use of public assistance by mother-headed families in certain neighborhoods—sometimes called "impacted ghettos"—is more important than the overall poverty rate itself. When many fragmented and over-stressed families are grouped together in unstable neighborhoods over extended periods, "underclass" behavior often emerges.[4] In this context, "underclass" means patterns of widely shared beliefs and actions in a neighborhood that run counter to accepted societal standards. There is no standardized definition of "underclass behavior," but commonly accepted indicators usually include persistent use of public assistance; substance abuse; long-term unemployment; early school-leaving and chronic truancy; early, unmarried pregnancies; absent, non-supporting fathers;

and high rates of delinquency and crime. Parents often have low aspirations, provide limited supervision for their children, and are prone to move frequently.[5]

While the causes and remedies for impacted ghettos remain under debate, the role of health, education and human service organizations in these neighborhoods is a question of central interest to state, county and city government. Not only do families and youth in areas of concentrated poverty typically experience multiple, serious and recurrent crises, but the current and future costs to society are high. It is unlikely that Detroit or any other urban community can sustain long-term redevelopment unless there is a reduction in the number of impacted ghettos. Economic development and education reform represent two widely accepted thrusts that must be undertaken. A third is management, remediation and prevention of social and emotional stresses that leave youth in these neighborhoods isolated, vulnerable, unsupported, and sometimes defeated before they reach adulthood.

KEY POLICY QUESTIONS

The role of health and human services in responding to the needs of Detroit and Wayne County's most challenged families must be more strategic and focused than at any time in the past three decades. Declining public resources, increasing competition in the private sector for available charitable gifts, lowered public confidence in expert interventions, and worsening social problems create a difficult climate for experimentation and traditional practice alike. Issues of service access, coordination, and targeting have now taken center stage as means for improving efficiency and outcomes.

Specifically, the central policy questions that must be addressed in a re-examination of health and human service organizations are:

- Who should receive services or care?
- Where should services or care be provided?
- Who should be involved in service planning and delivery?

These questions directly affect most of the issues and outcomes about which current policy debates are raging most furiously: cost, numbers of youth served, severity of problems addressed, neighborhood or community orientation, family focus, efficiency of service organization, and service outcomes.

CURRENT STATE OF AFFAIRS

In 1989 nearly 38 percent of all Detroit/Wayne County children and youth aged 0-17 were involved in one or more programs for at-risk youth. According to a study by the Children and Youth Initiative of Detroit/Wayne County, approximately 250,000 youngsters received one or more services or benefits related to health problems, substance abuse, inadequate housing or family income, mental illness, social or emotional problems, poor school functioning, and delinquency.[6] Despite the general perception that considerable overlap exists among programs, more than 85 percent of the children and youth in this survey were clients in only one or two programs during a 2-week survey period.[7]

The most frequently tapped resources for at-risk children were Aid to Families with Dependent Children and Food Stamps. These assistance programs alone affected 85 percent of all children and youth receiving any form of help. However, average benefits received by children were low, at only $186 per child per month. Specialized educational programs—such as Headstart, compensatory education, and services for the physically and emotionally handicapped—represented the second largest service category, involving 78,741 Wayne County children, 69 percent of whom lived in Detroit. Average costs per child were approximately $104, even lower than public assistance.[8]

While income and education programs for vulnerable children were the largest in terms of numbers served, the most costly programs per child were those in mental health, delinquency, child welfare, substance abuse, and health. However, program cost varied significantly depending on whether services were received by the child in a 24-hour setting such as a hospital, residential treatment center, or training school or in the community. Institutional forms of care or control accounted for nearly two-thirds (65 percent) of all costs. Cash assistance, food programs, and other forms of concrete aid to youth constituted only 19 percent of total expenditures, public or private, for Wayne County youth, ages 0-17.[9] All remaining community-based programs for at-risk youth in the health and human services combined consumed just 16 percent of dollars spent.

Examples of community-based, non-residential programs include such familiar services as substance abuse prevention, delinquency prevention, parent training groups, family counseling, out-patient mental health therapy, most employment and training programs for youth,

Table 1.
Estimated Combined Cost of Health and Human Service Programs Serving At-Risk Youth, Ages 0-17, by Service Setting, 2-Week Sample, Wayne County, 1989

Type of Benefit	Total 2-Week Cost	Average Cost	Total Served
Cash/Food Aid-Dollar Payment	$40,008,144	$181	220,549
24-Hour Institutional Care	4,244,156	630	6,736
Community-Based Clinics, In-Home Service, Day Programs	17,003,268	155	109,678

Table includes estimated dollar value of all cash payments, 24-hour care, and hours of direct service community programs provided to children and youth for an average 2-week period in Detroit/Wayne County. Costs were obtained through interviews by The Children and Youth Initiative of Detroit/Wayne County with a sample of 1,400 service providers in Wayne County in 1989-1990. Health care costs outside of hospitals and other 24-hour care facilities are not included, nor is subsidized public housing. Data include services and care provided through mental health, child welfare, delinquency programs, corrections, substance abuse, special education, public assistance (ADC, AFDC, SSI, GA), and youth employment and training.

family preservation and other in-home interventions, case management services, protective services, information and referral services, adoption counseling, legal services, home health visits, infant mental health services, services through community-based public health programs, and specialized education services in the schools. In short, these services reflect the full array of prevention, education, rehabilitation, information, and support services that are offered by the public and private sectors for the purpose of sustaining or enhancing the well-being of children and youth in their own natural environment.

Table 1 compares the relative costs for services, care, and cash payments received by children and youth during a sample two-week period in Detroit/Wayne County during 1989.

As table 1 shows, the cost of placing a child out of the home is almost twice as much as providing the same child with a combination of community-based services and cash or in-kind benefits. The discrepancy is even greater for some age groups, notably adolescents. An analysis of cost data by age shows that for the time period examined in table 1, the average amount of community-based service as measured by hours and dollar expenditures declined for children over age twelve in every human service sector except health.[10] At the same time, adolescents are highly vulnerable to institutionalization in the mental health, delinquency, and child welfare sectors. The push toward institutional options for care or control is more difficult to resist in the absence of adequately supported intensive services in the community.

Thus, despite the relatively greater media attention and policy debate devoted to cost and effectiveness of community services, the de facto policy supported by public expenditure in Detroit/Wayne County is a high rate of investment in out-of-home, out-of-community placements for children and youth. And despite the fact that adolescents present increasingly serious problems in almost every sphere of community functioning compared to the 1970s,[11] per capita spending for community-based interventions remains lower than for other age groups.

From the perspective of state and local finance, it has of course been widely recognized that the costs of institutional or out-of-home care and confinement per person greatly exceed other forms of home, office, or street-based intervention. Institutionalization is nevertheless often justified as necessary from the standpoint of public interest and, in many cases, in the interests of the client. Examples include treatment of violent, addicted, or uncontrollable delinquents, psychotic or other acutely ill children, and seriously maltreated or abandoned infants and youth.

If utilization of 24-hour care facilities were employed uniformly to address problems that greatly exceeded capacities of family and neighborhood resources, and removal were treated as a last resort, then relatively few children might be affected. There would generally be no discernible differences between children referred for 24-hour care by race or gender. On the other hand, if systematic biases do affect which children are removed from their families and neighborhoods, then there may be significant, undesirable social repercussions exceeding considerations of cost or immediate treatment outcomes.

Historically, there has been little reliable information on the extent to which systematic biases exist across the health and human services network in children's services at the local level. Program data are typically compiled by public and private agencies using different definitions of service, accounting periods, and client units for the purpose of reporting to very dissimilar monitoring authorities. Nevertheless, data from delinquency and child welfare programs point to the strong likelihood of selectivity for out-of home care by race.

It is known, for example, that non-white infants in Michigan enter foster care at three-and-a-half times the rate of white infants.[12] In 1985 more than 9600 abused and neglected children were in state-supervised out-of-home placements. By 1991 this number had reached nearly 13,000, and the cost had more than doubled.[13] In Wayne County, young African-American males were the most likely to be removed from their homes, a pattern consistent with national findings. African-American males continue to predominate among the 673 beds in residential treatment programs for delinquents under the supervision of the Michigan Department of Social Services.[14]

The most persuasive data for systematic bias in patterns of institutionalization across health and human service programs in Wayne County was collected by The Children and Youth Initiative of Detroit/Wayne County in 1989. In a comparison of mental health, child welfare, substance abuse, and delinquency programs for children and youth, 0-18, the Initiative found that African-American children were least likely to benefit from prevention and community-based programs. Table 2 shows the relative proportions receiving residential care or treatment among 19,705 Wayne County children or youth who obtained any form of service from public and private agencies during a representative 2-week period in 1989. (It should be noted that numbers of Hispanic, Asian American, Native American, and minorities other than African Americans represented less than 2 percent of all children in this group.) Data were obtained through reporting by front line staff of children actually seen or cared for during the sample survey, as opposed to caseloads assigned, data in agency records, or other more typical methods of service estimation.

Approximately 39 percent of all children and youth in Wayne County are African-American, but most are geographically concentrated in Detroit (77 percent of all residents age 17 or under).[15] As table 2 reflects, African-American children and youth are overrepresented in all human service programs, but their proportion in the institutional or other 24-hour out-of-home settings is particularly striking.

Table 2 shows that in mental health, child welfare, and delinquency programs, the percentage of African-American youth increased as intensity of care increased. For example, in the mental health sector, a little more than one-third of youth enrolled in individualized

Table 2.

Type of Care or Service Provided to Wayne County Children and Youth, Ages 0-17, by Race and Human Service Sector 2-Week Sample, Public and Private Agencies, 1989 (n=19,705)

RACE	HUMAN SERVICE SECTOR			
	Mental Health	Child Welfare	Delinquency Program	Substance Abuse[1]
Individualized Prevention and Education Programs[2]				
Afr. Amer.	36.6%	47.8%	68.3%	7.1%
White	26.8	41.0	28.2	92.9
Other	36.9	11.2	3.5	0.0
Counseling and Other Community-Based Programs[3]				
Afr. Amer.	55.4%	49.5%	69.1%	55.7%
White	39.0	48.6	28.7	41.5
Other	5.6	1.8	2.2	2.8
Residential Treatment and Care[4]				
Afr. Amer.	68.8%	74.3%	74.2%	0.0%
White	29.3	23.7	24.6	100.0
Other	1.9	2.0	1.1	0.0

1. The number of youth involved in substance abuse programs of any kind during the 2-week sample period was very small—only 467 individuals in all forms of treatment and prevention. The amount of substance abuse prevention programming in Detroit and Out-Wayne County has increased since 1989, with the availability of increased funding. However, it is estimated that as many as 100,000 young people in the tri-county Detroit area may need help for chemical dependency, so the shortfall in services is likely still to be great.
2. Includes *only* those prevention and education programs to which a high risk youth was specifically referred and for whom a record of participation was maintained by the organization. General school assemblies and other activities open to any child without screening or referral were omitted.
3. Includes out-patient mental health and substance abuse treatment, protective services, family counseling and therapy, case management services, probation services, diagnostic and assessment services, in-home programs such as family preservation services, respite care, day treatment, and adoption counseling.
4. Defined as 24-hour care or surveillance outside the home.

prevention and education programs were African American. This figure rose to more than half (55.4 percent) of those receiving out-patient counseling or other forms of community based counseling. Finally, of those in psychiatric hospitals[16] or other in-patient mental health facilities, more than two-thirds (68.8 percent) were African-American.

As table 2 reflects, child welfare programs in the community, including prevention and education, show the least bias by race when compared to mental health, delinquency programs, and substance abuse treatment. However, almost three-quarters of youth in residential care or custody in this sector were African-American. This is accounted for principally by higher placement rates of African-American youth in foster care. (Of 4,187 Wayne County youth receiving any form of child welfare service from public and private agencies during the 2-week survey period in 1989, the Initiative found that 3,092—73.8 percent—were African American.)

A second factor that appears to interact with race in influencing rates of residential or out-of-home care is gender. Males appear to be routed into different human service sectors more frequently than females, with further divergencies between pathways open to white males and African American males. As Table 3 shows, youth in the mental health, juvenile delinquency, and substance abuse sectors were predominantly male, according to the Children and Youth Initiative survey. Over four-fifths were age 10 or over.

The child welfare data are somewhat more complex. Males received more services from birth to age 2 and between ages 7-12. Females predominated after age 13. Thus, in effect, the child welfare system and public assistance system functioned as a primary source of service and protection for troubled or vulnerable young females, while the mental health, substance abuse, and delinquency systems were more central to problems of male youth.

A more detailed analysis of these same data shows that race again impacted services among males seventeen or under in the human service system. Proportionately more African-American males were shifted to the delinquency system, while mental health and substance abuse programs were more likely to assist white youth.[17] These patterns are highlighted in table 3.

The impact of institutionalization on the cost structure of human services, and the higher likelihood that African-American children and youth will be exposed to out-of-home placement, raise important policy questions. These questions are particularly crucial in relation to neighborhoods with high concentrations of poverty, where family fragmentation is already rife. A partial review of policy options suggests a number of alternative potential responses that might be made

Table 3.

Type of Care or Service Provided to Wayne County Children and Youth, Ages 0-17, by Gender and Human Service Sector 2-Week Sample, 1989 (n=19,705)

GENDER	HUMAN SERVICE SECTOR			
	Mental Health	Child Welfare	Delinquency Program	Substance Abuse[1]
Individualized Prevention and Education Programs				
Male	51.5%	48.6%	59.3%	51.4%
Female	48.5	51.4	40.7	48.6
Counseling and Other Community-Based Programs				
Male	64.7%	48.9%	85.8%	63.1%
Female	35.3	51.1	14.7	36.9
Residential Treatment and Other Out-of-Home Placement[1]				
Male	96.6%	47.4%	90.5%	100.0%
Female	3.4	52.6	9.5	0.0

1. Examples of residential treatment and other out-of-home placements include psychiatric facilities, juvenile detention and training centers, adult prisons, foster care, and in-patient detoxification programs.

by government and the private sector. The underlying assumption is that state and local initiatives rather than a national urban policy will constitute the most likely future platform for action.

POLICY OPTIONS

Improved training and information to reduce race and gender bias. There are many competing explanations for the higher likelihood that young males will be removed from home or community. Among school age children, males more frequently respond to stress or tension by becoming aggressive, while females tend to become depressed and are overlooked. Violent or poorly controlled behavior by young males, particularly as they move toward adolescence, has historically been treated by expulsion, institutionalization, or other forms of confinement. In the case of African-American children, some believe the problem is exacerbated by institutional racism. Threatening or deviant actions by African-American males have been even less tolerated in this society, stemming from roles and relationships established to maintain slavery.

If racial or ethnic stereotypes are in fact partly responsible for more pessimistic, severe, and controlling decisions affecting minority youth, then those involved in service planning and delivery must be given training and orientation designed to increase multi-cultural competence and sensitivity. This means, for example, expanded use of federal training funds (under Title IV-E of the Social Security Act) in child welfare and mental health programs to increase understanding of gender and race issues among current service providers.

In addition, at the systems level, new policies would be needed to facilitate the transfer of program and expenditure data between human service systems at the state and county levels. Service providers lack the means to review the consequences of their collective program decisions outside the framework of their own agencies. Most information systems have been constructed for the purpose of tracking financial information; program data have received secondary attention. Information system objectives therefore have lent themselves to multi-sector comparisons, vertical transfer of data from state to county service providers, or review in relation to key social variables in treatment, such as gender and race.

Expanded range of program options at the neighborhood or community level. A second explanation for continuing emphasis on institutionalization points more toward the lack of options within neighborhood and local service areas, particularly in communities characterized by concentrated poverty. Observers have suggested that over time, agencies and service programs migrate with the middle class away from the most deteriorated neighborhoods.[18] There is limited evidence that this may have happened in Detroit.[19] Obviously, if resources do not exist for a troubled child in his or her community, institutionalization or out-of-home treatment becomes the only alternative.

Methods for bringing a fuller range of services to the neighborhood have attracted the interest of policymakers since the beginning of the "War on Poverty" in 1962. "One-stop" service centers in some low-income neighborhoods were once supported. The erosion of public transportation systems has caused this idea to resurface. While attractive in its simplicity, there is, unfortunately, little evidence that co-location of services promotes either integration or improved access. Further, experience suggests that families living farther than 6-8 blocks from a neighborhood center tend not to participate. Perhaps more important than the structure of community services in seriously distressed neighborhoods is the question of who provides them.

Ultimately, public agencies such as the Michigan Department of Public Health, the Michigan Department of Social Services, local courts, and the Michigan Department of Mental Health have had responsibility, by default, for populations in greatest need. However, the distinction between public and private responsibilities has become blurred over the past two decades as a result of the purchase of service agreements and a renewed push toward privatization of some public functions. More recently, community activists have reasserted their interest in controlling the destinies of areas in which they live. Self-help, mutual aid, indigenous leadership, and volunteerism have reemerged as important themes in making neighborhoods more viable for children and youth.

A full spectrum of services in the most seriously stressed communities can be ensured only after the policy question has been resolved regarding who is to ensure equity in service distribution. If the private sector is to continue its major role in service provision—and this seems likely—then new mechanisms are needed that help this sector improve its accountability for overall social outcomes of service.

Timely service intervention. Society may continue to rely on institutional care, because some children are simply overlooked or helped only minimally until it is too late. Service interventions and community support mechanisms may not be adequately focused on the critical points at which children and youth become vulnerable to breakdown. Consequently, they are older and their problems are much more serious by the time their needs and problems are identified. At this point, draconian measures to protect child and community—including removal from home—may be necessary or at least seen as increasingly desirable from society's point of view.

This general argument is supported in part by data from The Children and Youth Initiative 1989 survey. Detailed analysis of the amount of service received by age, type of program, and number of at-risk youth served for a sample 2-week period points to declining levels of service in almost every sector for youth ages 6-11. Child welfare programs were most intensively utilized by children ages 0-6 and 12-17. Youth in mental health programs were found at ages as young as 7 or 8, and some clinics had initiated infant mental health demonstration programs. However, despite interesting and even exciting program features, the number of youth and infants affected remains small in comparison to total youth in the mental health system. Most mental health services were provided to youth ages 13 or over. Similarly, delinquency programs were most heavily focused on adolescents, as were substance abuse services. "Latency age" youth were not ignored in the human service system, but they received little attention in individualized programs for at-risk youth compared to pre-schoolers and teenagers.[20]

Inadequate service coordination. A fourth argument for the persistence of institutional care or out-of-home placement is the difficulty faced by agencies and families in providing long term, consistent support drawing upon a wide array of public, private and neighborhood resources. The culprit is in part the absence of mechanisms for service coordination, service development, and service termination. These mechanisms are lacking or inconsistently developed at the systems level not only within individual sectors such as mental health or child welfare, but between sectors. It should be noted that the Michigan Department of Social Services has over the past five years gradually broadened its concept of "family preservation." Case management and case coordination through such child welfare programs as Families First and multi-sector demonstrations such as the Michigan Family Preservation Initiative (MIFPI) aim at greater fluidity of service across traditional boundaries. The Michigan Department of Mental Health and the Department of Public Health have interested themselves in similar experimentation.

At the present time, the concepts of "case coordination," "case management," "service integration," "collaboration," and "cooperation" have been used in many ways. Most effective community-oriented providers would legitimately claim they already have many points of planned interaction with other organizations. The central policy issue is, however, whether these agreements and interconnections result in reduced days of care in institutions, reduced hours of intervention with families over time, and produce greater intensity of involvement by appropriate organizations at points of crisis among families and youth most susceptible to disorganization. Many current multi-sector agreements would not meet this test.

SUMMARY

Revitalization of urban neighborhoods in cities such as Detroit is inextricably linked to the stability and future productivity of the youth who reside there. Areas of highly-concentrated poverty are perhaps the most resistant to rejuvenation, partly because successful role models have left and racial segregation leaves families isolated from the broader culture. The role of human services in these neighborhoods has special meaning, because so many connecting links between individuals and community are under attack by broader forces of economic infrastructure change, demographic shifts, and value uncertainty.

Data from a Children and Youth Initiative survey of Detroit/Wayne County in 1989 have been used to illustrate the combined service patterns of mental health, substance abuse, child welfare, and delinquency programs for a 2-week survey period. The data reveal a pattern of continuing over-investment in institutional confinement and residential treatment compared to cash transfers and community-based services. The pattern is particularly observable for African American male youth. The impact of de facto policies that disproportionately remove some children from their homes and not others is serious, particularly in neighborhoods with low resilience and the highest rates of poverty.

Several policy options may be considered as a means of reducing undesirable high rates of out-of-home care. Improved training and information for service providers to reduce race and gender bias in case planning is one alternative. A second is an expanded range of program options at the neighborhood or community level to reduce the necessity for removal. A third option is more timely service intervention before problems become irremediable at home. This would include not only prevention but increased resources for treatment in neighborhood-based facilities. Finally, a re-designed mechanism for public and private sector service coordination might reduce the present inconsistency in service interventions over time and address multiple family needs simultaneously, rather than in sequence. This would create a more favorable context in the home for solution of problems affecting children and youth.

The common theme among all four options discussed in this paper is the need for invention of new mechanisms that allow for multi-sector service overviews, multi-sector service tracking, and multi-sector

accountability for service outcomes. A second theme is improved spec-
ification of public and private sector roles. The resolution of these
issues will help to determine whether high-need youth can become a
positive part of their community's future.

NOTES

1. These include San Jose and Oakland, California; Fort Lauderdale, Florida;
   Honolulu, Hawaii; Buffalo and the Borough of Bronx, New York; Columbus
   and Cincinnati, Ohio; Seattle, Washington; Pittsburgh, Pennsylvania; Fort
   Worth, Texas. Thirty-three states currently have no municipal center over
   800,000. The State of Connecticut has no independent municipalities, and
   the cities of Denver, Baltimore, San Francisco, Philadelphia, St. Louis, and
   the District of Columbia are independent of county government.
2. Marilyn L. Flynn, et al., *Children and Youth Initiative Survey, 1989: Executive
   Summary* (Detroit: The Children and Youth Initiative of Detroit/Wayne
   County, April 1990). This includes all health care, substance abuse, housing,
   emergency shelter, mental health, child welfare, and delinquency programs
   offering direct services, care, or cash payments to at-risk youth in the
   county.
3. Ibid.; Data were based on a customized search of files by the Michigan
   Department of Social Services.
4. William Julius Wilson, *The Declining Significance of Race: Blacks and Changing
   American Institutions,* 2nd ed. (Chicago: University of Chicago, 1980). See
   also, by the same author: *The American Underclass: Inner City Ghettos and the
   Norms of Citizenship* (Cambridge, Massachusetts: John F. Kennedy School of
   Government, Harvard University Godkin Lecture Series, April 1988). See
   also, Mark Alan Hughes, "Misspeaking Truth to Power: A Geographical
   Perspective on the 'Underclass' Fallacy," Princeton University, unpublished
   paper, January, 1989.
5. Loic J. D. Wacquant and William Julius Wilson, "Poverty, Joblessness and
   the Social Transformation of the Inner City," in *Welfare Policy for the 1990s,*
   edited by Phoebe H. Cottingham and David T. Ellwood (Cambridge,
   Massachusetts: Harvard University, 1989). See also, Loic J. D. Wacquant and
   William Julius Wilson, "The Cost of Racial and Class Exclusion in the Inner
   City," *Annuals of the American Academy of Political Science and Social Science*
   501 (January 1989):14-25.
6. Flynn et al., *Children.*
7. The Children and Youth Initiative Database, Michigan State University,
   School of Social Work.
8. Cost estimates provided through databases for Special Education and
   Headstart maintained by the Wayne County Intermediate School District
   (now the Wayne County Regional Educational Services Agency); the Office
   of Research and Evaluation of the Detroit Public Schools Chapter 1/Article 3
   database; the Office of Information Systems of the Detroit Public Schools

Special Education database and Bilingual database; and the Michigan Department of Education Chapter 1 database. Figures represent combined costs for very different programs. Compensatory education projects vary between schools and usually are limited to reading and math tutoring, while special education programs range from full-day alternative classrooms to specialized schools serving children with complex physical and developmental needs.

9. Sources: Michigan Department of Social Services Medicaid, Aid to Families with Dependent Children, Supplemental Social Security Income and General Assistance databases; Wayne County Community Mental Health Board; Detroit Bureau of Substance Abuse; Southeastern Michigan Substance Abuse Services; Michigan Department of Corrections; Wayne County Court; Children and Youth Initiative Survey, 1989.

10. M. Flynn, *Preliminary Survey of Survey Results* (Detroit: The Children and Youth Initiative of Detroit/Wayne County, 1990). It should be noted that the volume of service is greatest in Wayne County for children 0-5 and 13-17. In the case of adolescents, more clients receive increasingly less attention, especially after age sixteen.

11. National Commission on Children, *Beyond Rhetoric: A New American Agenda for Children and Families* (Washington, D.C.: U.S. Government Printing Office, 1991).

12. Center for the Study of Youth Policy, *Child Welfare and Delinquency Trends in Michigan, 1981-1990* (Ann Arbor: University of Michigan, School of Social Work, Center for the Study of Youth Policy, 1991 May).

13. Michigan Department of Social Services, February 1992, as cited in J. Abbey, *A Chorus: Themes for Michigan's Child Welfare System* (Detroit: The Skillman Foundation, January 1993).

14. Office of Delinquency Services/Residential Care Division, *Annual Report* (Lansing: Michigan Department of Social Services, March 1992).

15. Estimates based on 1990 census data, which may slightly underrepresent the number of African Americans in Detroit.

16. The study does not include data on children or youth in private, for-profit facilities.

17. Marilyn L. Flynn, *Final Report to the Youth Advisory Commission, Detroit City Council* (Detroit: The Children and Youth Initiative of Detroit/Wayne County, May 1990). See also, The Children and Youth Initiative of Detroit/Wayne County, *Social Services/Housing/Income Support Sector Briefing Session* (Detroit: The Children and Youth Initiative, February 1990).

18. See Wilson, *The Declining Significance of Race*. Data from The Children and Youth Initiative survey suggest, for example, that private agencies may be more heavily concentrated on the west side of Detroit which is relatively more affluent. This leaves public agencies such as the Department of Social Services with overwhelming responsibility for services in the city's most distressed neighborhoods on the east side.

19. Flynn, *Final Report*. Data show significant differences in service utilization on the east and west sides of Detroit by auspice of provider. Private providers were more concentrated on the relatively more affluent west side.

20. Children and Youth Initiative of Detroit/Wayne County, *Mental Health*

Sector Briefing Session (Detroit: Children and Youth Initiative, March 1990); Children and Youth Initiative of Detroit/Wayne County, *Social Services;* Children and Youth Initiative of Detroit/Wayne County, *Health and Substance Abuse Sector Briefing Session* (Detroit: The Children and Youth Initiative, April 1990). Children and Youth Initiative of Detroit/Wayne County, *Juvenile Justice Sector Briefing Session* (Detroit: Children and Youth Initiative, January 1990).

About the Contributors

JANET BOKEMEIER

Janet Bokemeier is a professor of sociology at Michigan State University with a special appointment as Coordinator for State Issues Response Initiatives. She is a rural sociologist with special research interests in work, family and gender issues in rural America. Her current research program involves studies of children's experiences with poverty in rural Michigan, the impact of changes in the dairy industry for farm families and rural communities, and multiple jobholding and underemployment in non-metropolitan households. Dr. Bokemeier has published extensively, with articles appearing in the *Journal of Marriage and the Family, Rural Sociology, Journal of Extension, Family Relations* and elsewhere. She is currently co-author of a book, *Harvest of Hope: Farm Families and Family Farming,* that is under contract with the University of Kentucky Press.

MARILYN FLYNN

Marilyn Flynn is a professor and Director of the School of Social Work at Michigan State University. She received her Ph.D. from the University of Illinois at Urbana-Champaign in 1976 and has since specialized in social administration, planning and program design. She has acted as consultant to more than 50 federal, state and local organizations and has served on the faculties of the University of Illinois, the University of Michigan, Wayne State University, and Michigan State

University. Her current interests include research and teaching on children, youth and families, development of multi-sector coalitions for service delivery to high-risk families, and comparative international studies of family care systems.

STUART H. GAGE

Stuart H. Gage is a professor in the Department of Entomology at Michigan State University. Dr. Gage's research focuses on quantitative ecological investigations of insects and their hosts. A primary emphasis is on the interrelationships of insects and weather as well as landscape features, with a goal of forecasting insect populations and assessing risk over large geographic areas. The effect of intercropping systems on insect populations is an evolving emphasis. He teaches a course on biological information systems. Dr. Gage directs the Entomology Spatial Analysis Laboratory, which has an array of geographic information systems technology. He received his Ph.D. from MSU in 1974.

PHYLLIS T. H. GRUMMON

Phyllis T. H. Grummon is an assistant professor in the College of Education in the Department of Educational Administration at Michigan State University. She holds a research appointment with the Institute for Research on Teaching Adults, where she focuses on research related to the transition from school to work and education in the workplace. Dr. Grummon is also a faculty affiliate at the Institute for Public Policy and Social Research. She serves on a number of national panels related to workforce readiness and has developed assessments for that area. She has written a number of papers on the transition from school to work and the assessment of workforce readiness.

CRAIG K. HARRIS

Craig K. Harris is currently an associate professor in the Department of Sociology at Michigan State University, where he works in the areas of environmental sociology and the sociology of agriculture. He is particularly interested in the relationships linking agriculture and the

environment, and has conducted many studies of farmers' consideration of environmental factors in making decisions about farming
methods. He directed a survey of Michigan fruit growers for the Status
and Potential of Michigan Agriculture Project, and is currently directing a study of factors which affect the transition to low-input sustainable production methods.

DIANE HOLT-REYNOLDS

Diane Holt-Reynolds is an assistant professor of teacher education
with the College of Education at Michigan State University. She is a
senior researcher with the National Center for Research on Teacher
Learning. Her projects there include a longitudinal study of how
undergraduate English majors develop disciplinary understanding and
teaching expertise and a second research study focusing on the content and character of preservice teachers' beliefs about teaching and
learning and the changes in those beliefs as they develop professional
knowledge. Dr. Holt-Reynolds received her Ed.D. in Curriculum and
Teaching with an emphasis in subject matter-specific literacy instruction from the University of Michigan in 1990. She worked in a public
high school in southern Indiana teaching English and theater arts for
13 years.

STEPHEN S. KAAGAN

Stephen S. Kaagan is professor of education at the College of Education,
Michigan State University, with assignments in Educational
Administration and University Extension. Previously he served as chief
state education officer (Vermont, 1982-1988), academic head of an institution of higher education (Pratt Institute, 1977-1982), and chief executive of a non-profit educational organization (Hurricane Island Outward
Bound, 1989-1991). He has been a classroom teacher (Arlington,
Massachusetts and Canberra, Australia) and has taught management
and organization development at Pratt Institute, Rutgers University, and
the University of Southern Maine. Dr. Kaagan has a doctorate from
Harvard and a bachelor's from Williams College, as well as two hon-
orary degrees (Williams College and Green Mountain College in
Vermont.)

JEAN KAYITSINGA

Jean Kayitsinga is a doctoral candidate and research assistant in the Department of Sociology at Michigan State University. His major is in rural sociology with particular interests in rural families and demography. He has a special interest in demographic methods and statistical methodologies. His master's thesis is entitled "Livelihood Strategies Among Farm Youth in Rwanda." He participated in the 1992-1993 Fellows Program in Population Policies at the Population Research Bureau, where he published "The Duration of Breast-Feeding in Burundi."

BETTIE LANDAUER-MENCHIK

Bettie Landauer-Menchik is a research associate at the Institute for Public Policy and Social Research at Michigan State University. Her research is in the fields of poverty analysis and changes in families and children within Michigan. She is responsible for all the data in the *Kids Count in Michigan Databook*. Another research interest is in how to assist students and community organizations to learn to use statistical information for program planning and evaluation and for community analysis.

DEBORAH G. MCCULLOUGH

Deborah G. McCullough is an assistant professor in the Departments of Entomology and Forestry at Michigan State University. She is involved in research, teaching, and extension activities related to forest entomology. Dr. McCullough currently conducts research on the effects of the gypsy moth on native insect biodiversity and on an endangered butterfly species, and is evaluating two biological control agents of the gypsy moth. She also directs the Michigan Gypsy Moth Education Program and works with state and federal forest management agencies to oversee gypsy moth management in Michigan. Other areas of research include management of Christmas tree insect pests and the effects of insect defoliation on jack pine ecosystems. Dr. McCullough received her M.S.F. in forestry from Northern Arizona University. She obtained her Ph.D. in entomology from the University of Minnesota in 1990 and was employed by the USDA Forest Service prior to arriving at Michigan State University.

PAUL MENCHIK

Paul Menchik is professor of economics and currently is chairperson of the Economics Department at Michigan State University. He received his Ph.D. at the University of Pennsylvania in 1976. His fields of specialization are public finance and income distribution, and he is both widely published and frequently cited in these areas. He was on the faculty of the University of Wisconsin before coming to MSU and has been an academic visitor at Stanford University, The London School of Economics, and the University of Pennsylvania. Menchik has advised several state governments and has most recently served the federal government as senior economist for economic policy at the Office of Management and Budget in Washington.

BRENDAN MULLAN

Brendan Mullan is a demographer who teaches in the Department of Sociology and is Director of the Michigan Database unit within the Institute for Public Policy and Social Research at Michigan State University. Dr. Mullan holds a Ph.D. from the University of Pennsylvania. Prior to joining MSU, he spent two years as a research associate at the University of Oxford in England. He specializes in socio-economic demographic research, with a current emphasis on the causes and consequences of international migration and related processes of assimilation and adaptation. With the United Nations Economic Commission for Europe, he is currently undertaking research into the channels, content and consequences of international migration from the countries of Eastern Europe. In addition, he has an active research agenda focusing on the population of Michigan. He coedited *Policy Choices,* vol. 1 (East Lansing: Michigan State University Press, 1993) which highlights some of the major policy issues and choices facing Michigan. He recently completed three papers analyzing data on Michigan rural community leadership, collected in early 1993. This research seeks to describe, explore, and assess rural communities, the issues and problems confronting rural community leaders in Michigan, and how these can be addressed by policymakers at all levels.

NIGEL PANETH

Nigel Paneth is professor of Pediatrics and Epidemiology and director of the Program in Epidemiology at Michigan State University. His research has been on infant mortality and childhood handicap, with the emphasis on prevention. Currently his work focuses on better understanding the causes and consequences of brain damage in premature infants.

BRYAN C. PIJANOWSKI

Bryan C. Pijanowski is an assistant visiting professor in the Department of Entomology at Michigan State University. Dr. Pijanowski's research focuses on spatial analysis of gypsy moth population dynamics with respect to landscape features. He is currently participating in a statewide project to investigate how different pest management strategies can be employed to slow the spread of the gypsy moth in Michigan's Upper Peninsula. Other areas of research include field research and modeling of the relationships between insect abundance and the growth and development of altricial birds. Recent research has also focused on interdisciplinary projects that involve how computer technology can be used to provide policy analysts with information about the interactions of biological, earth, and human social factors related to the causes and effects of global environmental change. Dr. Pijanowski is an active member of MSU's Entomology Spatial Analysis Laboratory.

MARK E. WHALON

Mark E. Whalon, professor of entomology at Michigan State University and agricultural science leader, has been involved in applied ecological research since 1976. Areas of study include integrated pest management, resistance management, and application of biotechnology diagnostics to agricultural pest management. This work has led to the abatement of pesticides in the environment in Michigan, nationally, and internationally. Dr. Whalon is recognized as a world authority on the evolutionary adaptation of pests to various mechanisms of control. He speaks and teaches widely. In addition, he serves on the executive committee of the International Organization for World Pest Resistance Management and is editor and chief publisher of the Resistant Pest Management Newsletter, to which 2600 scientists and policymakers from 32 countries subscribe. Representatives from 14 countries and 10 states attended his Global Pest Resistance Management Summer Institute.

Index

A

African-American youth, out-of-home care, 195-97
Agricultural Experiment Station (1887), 90
Agriculture Experiment Station (AES) at MSU, 132
Aid to Families with Dependent Children (AFDC), 47, 192
Apprenticeships, 176, 179

B

Business: and education and training program, 181

C

Carl D. Perkins Act, 175
Child welfare services: African American children, 197; male vs. female, 197
Children and Youth Initiative of Detroit/Wayne County, 190, 195
Community activists, 200
Community-based programs, 192-93

Cooperative Extension Service, 90
Cost of health and human service programs serving at-risk youth, *193*

D

Demographic overview of labor market areas in Michigan, *50*
Disease prevention, 42
Diversity in produce, 105
DNR, see Michigan Department of Natural Resources (MDNR)

E

Education policy: making policy, changing schools, 164-65; comparisons with other areas of endeavor, 168-69; student learning means teacher learning, 165-68; policy options to support more effective teaching, 169-70; policymaking; binding agreements, 163; capacity building, 163; incentives, 163; influential